Joh. Seb. Bach.

Basically BACH®

A 300th Birthday Celebration

Herbert Kupferberg

McGraw-Hill Book Company

New York   St. Louis   San Francisco
Toronto   Hamburg   Mexico

To the memory of Lorna Kasarsky

"Basically Bach" ® Musica Sacra of New York

"Edifying Thoughts of a Tobacco Smoker," on page 111: Reprinted from THE BACH READER, A Life of Johann Sebastian Bach in Letters and Documents, edited by Hans T. David and Arthur Mendel, by permission of W. W. Norton & Company, Inc. Copyright © 1966, 1945 by W. W. Norton & Company, Inc.

1 2 3 4 5 6 7 8 9 F G R F G R 8 7 6 5

ISBN 0-07-035646-7

LIBRARY OF CONGRESS CATALOGING IN PUBLICATION DATA

Kupferberg, Herbert.
Basically Bach.
1. Bach, Johann Sebastian, 1685–1750—Anniversaries, etc., 1985. I. Title.
ML410.B1K85 1985   780′.92′4   84-26084
ISBN 0-07-035646-7

Book design by Patrice Fodero

Contents

Contents

Prelude

"Say what you like, but for God's sake, don't tell us anything about Bach in B minor."

—T. P. O'Connor, editor of the *London Star*, upon hiring George Bernard Shaw as a music critic in 1888.

This book will not tell you anything about Bach in B minor.

I first got the idea of writing it some years ago when I was working on a biography of Felix Mendelssohn and his family. It was Mendelssohn who, in 1829, revived the *Passion According to St. Matthew*, which had gone unperformed for 100 years, and thereby rescued Johann Sebastian Bach from the near oblivion to which he and his music had fallen.

Mendelssohn's assistant and abettor in this project was a part-time singer, part-time actor named Eduard Devrient. After their successful performance, Mendelssohn, who was all of 20 years old, exclaimed to Devrient: "To think that an actor and a Jew should give back to the people the greatest Christian music in the world!"

The remark—which Devrient said was the only time Mendelssohn ever referred in his hearing to his Jewish origin—illustrates vividly the universality of Johann Sebastian Bach, who spent his entire existence within a narrow geographical compass of Germany, worshipped as a faithful Lutheran, earned his living as a local musician and schoolmaster, and yet reaches out to people of all nations, faiths, occupations, and interests.

The 300th anniversary of Bach's birth, in 1685, is being observed around the world with concerts, festivals, special performances, and celebrations of various sorts. Amid all these large events I hope there will be room for a small book that attempts to treat Bach from a different aspect—through sidelights, anecdotes, lists, reflections, opinions, and other incidental information and data from his own time to the present.

Bach was in the habit of titling his works with a diminutive, *The Little Organ Book*, *The Little Clavier Book*, and the like, and then filling them with masterpieces. This little book aspires to no such attainment, but I hope that from its pages will emerge a clear and convincing portrait of the human being and genius who produced a music that has not been surpassed in three centuries.

Bach and the Cosmos

f and when a spacecraft named *Voyager* lands on a remote world it will greet the inhabitants thereof—if any— with the music of the first movement of Bach's Brandenburg Concerto No. 2 in F. Actually there are two such spacecraft, *Voyager I* and *Voyager II*, launched in 1977 on a course that will take them through the solar system and beyond, to the realm of the stars. Among the devices with which each has been equipped is a gold-coated phonograph record containing an hour and a half of music, in addition to spoken greetings. The music includes three pieces by Bach: the first movement of the Brandenburg Concerto No. 2 in F (which opens the record), the Prelude and Fugue in C from Book II of *The Well-Tempered Clavier*, and the Gavotte en Rondeaux from the

Partita No. 3 for Unaccompanied Violin. The Brandenburg concerto was chosen as the first music from earth to be heard because of its feeling of "energetic optimism."

Carl Sagan, the eminent astronomer and writer, reports that when he asked biologist Lewis Thomas of the Sloan-Kettering Institute what message he thought should be sent to other civilizations in space, Dr. Thomas replied: "I would send the complete works of Johann Sebastian Bach." Then he paused and added: "But that would be boasting."

In any event, the three pieces by Bach, as well as excerpts from Beethoven, Mozart, and others, are on their way. The *Voyagers*, if all go well, are scheduled to fly past Uranus in 1986 and Neptune in 1989 and then proceed beyond. The ships are equipped with record-playing equipment and instructions engraved in aluminum in scientific language that any reasonable space creature should be able to follow. We await word.

The Sayings of J. S. Bach

ach himself was not a man of many words, yet he expressed himself with pith, vigor, and honesty—characteristics that also mark his music. When the occasion called for it, as in inscribing a dedication, he could adopt courtly phraseology. But most of his recorded opinions are terse and to the point. Here are some of his sentiments on a variety of subjects.

"I was obliged to work hard; whoever works equally hard will succeed equally well."
—Quoted by J. N. Forkel in the first Bach biography.

"When the air of Leipzig is wholesome there are fewer funerals."

> —Letter to a friend complaining about decline in his fees from officiating at funeral services.

"The ultimate end of thoroughbass should only be the glory of God and the recreation of the mind. Where these are not kept in view there can be no real music, only an infernal jingling and bellowing."

> —Rules on thoroughbass (harmonic composition) written in an informal instructional manual.

"You should have been a shoemaker!"

> —Shouted at an organist who made a mistake during a rehearsal at St. Thomas's Church in Leipzig. Arturo Toscanini used the same term in scolding musicians at the New York Philharmonic, flinging down his watch as he did so. Bach is recorded as flinging down his wig.

"I consider my [musical] parts as if they were persons who converse together like a select company."

> —Reported by Forkel.

"When a musician has to worry about his bread, he cannot think of improving, much less distinguishing himself."

> —Report to the Leipzig Town Council, asking higher pay for his performers.

THE SAYINGS OF J. S. BACH

"Indeed it is a pity that in so noble a gift of God the smallest drop should have been wasted."

> —Letter to a cousin who had sent him a cask of wine that developed a leak in transit.

"Above all, I must know whether an organ has good lungs."

> —Observation when about to try out a new instrument.

"You tune the organ the way you please, and I play the organ in the key I please."

> —Remark to Gottfried Silbermann, piano and organ builder.

"There is nothing remarkable about it. All you have to do is hit the right key at the right time and the instrument plays itself."

> —Reply when complimented upon his organ playing.

"Just practice diligently, and it will go very well. You have five fingers on each hand just as healthy as mine."

> —Remark to a pupil.

"Everything has to be possible."

> —Indicating no task is beyond accomplishment. Reported by J. F. Kirnberger, a former pupil.

Bach: Pro and Con

"This great man would be the admiration of whole nations if he had more amenity, if he did not deprive his pieces of their naturalness by giving them a bombastic and confused style, and if he did not obscure their beauty by too much art."

> —Johann Adolf Scheibe, 1737. Scheibe, a composer and organist, was Bach's most persistent critic during his lifetime. Bach had once adjudicated a competition in which Scheibe had lost.

"Departed Bach! Long since thy splendid organ playing
Alone brought thee the noble cognomen 'The Great.'

And what thy pen had writ, the highest art
   displaying,
Did some with joy and some with envy contemplate."
> —Georg Philipp Telemann, 1751. Praise
> from a contemporary.

"Bach, sir? Bach's concert? And pray, sir, who is Bach?
Is he a piper?"
> —Dr. Samuel Johnson. The query is
> reported by Fanny Burney in *Memoirs of
> Dr. Burney*. The allusion may be to
> Bach's son, Johann Christian, who was
> active in England, but Dr. Johnson
> undoubtedly would have extended it to
> the father as well.

"Let *The Well-Tempered Clavier* be your daily bread.
Then you certainly will become a solid musician."
> —Robert Schumann. From his *House
> Maxims for Young Musicians, 1848*.

"It was heart-rending, I assure you, to see three such
admirable talents, full of fire, brilliant in youthful
vitality, united in a bundle to reproduce this ridiculous
and stupid psalmody."
> —Hector Berlioz. After hearing a Bach
> concerto for three pianos played by
> Frederic Chopin, Franz Liszt, and
> Ferdinand Hiller.

"In Bach there is too much crude Christianity, crude
Germanism, crude scholasticism. He stands at the

threshold of modern European music, but he is always looking back toward the Middle Ages."

—Friedrich Nietzsche, 1878.

"Sebastian Bach was of a strong, self-willed race, and the conflicts with the authorities in which he was always finding himself lead one to suspect that this violent man was hard to live with."

—Wilhelm Dilthey. A nineteenth-century German philosopher's opinion. No complaints from Bach's family have been recorded on this score.

"Bravo for Bach!"

—Georges Bizet. Comment by the future composer of *Carmen*, who had been called upon to judge a fugue-writing contest in 1872.

"I like to play Bach, because it is interesting to play a good fugue; but I do not regard him, in common with many others, as a great genius."

—Peter Ilyich Tchaikovsky. Diary, 1886.

"This benevolent God to whom musicians should pray before starting on their own work to guard themselves from mediocrity."

—Claude Debussy. *La Revue S.I.M.*, Paris, 1913.

"With my prying nose I dipped into all composers, and found that the houses they erected were stable in the exact proportion that Bach was used in the foundation."

—James Huneker. *Old Fogy*, 1913.

"I used to say, 'Bach is the first composer with twelve tones.' This was a joke, of course. . . . But the truth on which this statement is based is that Fugue No. 24 of *The Well-Tempered Clavier*, in B minor, begins with a *Dux* [theme] in which all twelve tones appear."

—Arnold Schoenberg, 1950.

"The miracle of Bach has not appeared in any other art. . . . I don't deny that Bach is a German master, but it is a mistake to try and restrict him with a national label. . . . He is among those geniuses who shine over all nations and all times."

—Pablo Casals. *Conversations with Casals*, 1956.

"While there undoubtedly were geniuses before Bach, we start our chain of immortals with him, and call no composers immortals before him."

—Carlos Chavez. *Musical Thought*, 1961.

"Bach's works are the Reformation put to music."

—Will Durant. *The Age of Voltaire*, 1965.

"He taught how to find originality within an established discipline; actually—how to live."

—Jean-Paul Sartre. Quoted in *Time* magazine, December 27, 1968.

Zimmermann's Coffee House

ne can meet Bach, historically speaking, in many locales—on Sunday in church playing the organ or directing his latest cantata; in a ducal court demonstrating his prowess as a clavier performer; in school teaching a class music or Latin; at home deeply immersed in the affairs and problems of a large and rapidly growing family.

But rather than at any of these places, it might have been especially enjoyable to encounter him at an institution called Zimmermann's Coffee House—the early eighteenth-century equivalent of your friendly neighborhood tavern.

Zimmermann's, which was located at 14 Catherine Street in Leipzig, has never enjoyed the reputation of such other centers of artistic conviviality as the Mermaid Tavern of Elizabethan London or the Café des Deux Magots of modern Paris, but its contribution to cultural history is scarcely less imposing. For to Zimmermann's every Friday evening from 8 to 10 repaired Johann Sebastian Bach to conduct an assemblage of young musicians for the entertainment of the customers. The orchestral group was called a *Collegium Musicum*—the equivalent of our *musical society*—and had been originally established by Georg Philipp Telemann, the well-known composer who had preceded Bach to Leipzig.

Zimmermann's had competition, for there were two rival groups playing in town, one at an establishment called the Three Swans, the other at Schellhafer's Hall. But Zimmermann's customers must surely have had the best deal, for not only was Bach on hand but also he usually brought along two or three of his sons to join in the musical festivities.

These weekly performances, presented by the genial proprietor of the coffee house, Gottfried Zimmermann, were the closest Bach ever came to giving public concerts. Indeed, public concerts, with paid admissions, were just about unknown in the Germany of the time; at Zimmermann's, Bach, without knowing it, was helping to usher in the new era of public music making that was about to dawn.

What sort of music was performed at Zimmermann's? To begin with, there were student songs, because most of the musicians and many of the listeners were students at the University of Leipzig or one of the town's other schools. But the musical fare also undoubtedly included Bach's own compositions, such works as the Brandenburg concertos and the suites for orchestra, not to mention the harpsichord concertos, with Bach and his sons as solo performers. It's also believed that Bach's *Phoebus and Pan*—the closest he ever came to writing an opera—was presented at Zimmermann's, as well as, naturally enough, his *Coffee Cantata*, a charming work in praise of what was then a relatively new beverage (see Bach and the Opera).

Zimmermann's Coffee House had a regular local clientele, which was augmented by outside visitors during the Leipzig Fair. Indeed many merchants and travelers made the acquaintance of Johann Sebastian Bach not directing religious performances from the organ of St. Thomas's but presiding over a collection of eager and enthusiastic young musicians in the smoky, noisy coffee house.

The performers, in accordance with the custom of the time, were all male, with boy sopranos and altos participating along with the tenors and the basses. But women guests appear to have been scattered among the male onlookers and imbibers gathered at the tables. We have the testimony of a Leipzig poet named Mariane von Ziegler, obviously one of the more advanced women of her day. Mariane not only came to the Zimmermann's concerts, but she outspokenly complained about the way the young musicians were paid: "Most of the listeners seem to think that these sons of the Muse just extemporize the music. The reward they get is very poor indeed, and often they have to be content with a bare bone to pick for all the hours of preparation they put in."

Bach, it would seem, was paid far better than his musicians; as much as he enjoyed these musical outings he would hardly have continued as long as he did had he not received a substantial stipend for organizing and running the concerts.

In the summertime the Friday evening concerts moved out of doors to a garden owned by Zimmermann near Grimm's Gate—a pleasant locale where the tobacco smoke could dissipate readily on the evening breezes. Zimmermann served not only coffee but also plenty of beer, wine, and light snacks.

"Pops" concerts are by no means a twentieth-century invention.

Zimmermann himself died in 1741, and though the concerts continued, Bach, who was now in his fifties, turned them over to other hands. Perhaps he missed the old host, or perhaps he had too many other things to do. Eventually the place closed down.

Coffee house entertainment has never been the same.

All in the Family

he Bach family tree produced musicians as readily as an apple tree produces apples. In fact, it's doubtful that any family in any sphere of human activity has brought forth as distinguished a progeny as the Bachs.

Heredity and environment both played their parts. For several centuries virtually all the Bachs grew up in musical households, and most of them displayed an uncommon grasp of the musical art from the start. Altogether we know of some 400 Bachs between 1550 and 1850, of whom nearly sixty held important musical posts either as composers or performers. Johann Sebastian, incomparably the greatest, himself had four sons who became celebrated musicians. They constituted a family guild.

Eisenach, Bach's birthplace, in the middle of the seventeenth century.

The Bachs as a clan were proud of their distinction and that the name "Bach" had literally become synonymous with "musician." At regular intervals the clan would assemble in a specified town—Erfurt, Eisenach, and Arnstadt were among the locales—for a family gathering. As many as 125 different Bachs would attend these meetings, which continued to be held until the late eighteenth century.

Johann Sebastian was a fourth-generation Bach—that is, the names of four direct ancestors are known, dating back to the first musician in the family, Veit (or Vitus) Bach. Here is the father-son line leading to Johann Sebastian Bach:

Veit (or Vitus) Bach (1555–1619)
A baker by trade; his avocation was playing the zither.

Hans Bach (ca. 1580–1626)
A carpet weaver, he was known as *Der Spielmann* (the minstrel) because of his musical skills. He had a brother Lips Bach (d. 1620) who also was a musician. The name Lips was a diminutive of Philippus. So far as is known, Lips Bach was not a trumpet player.

Christoph Bach (1613–1661)
Stadtpfeifer (town musician; literally, town piper) in several cities, including Weimar. Sebastian Bach's paternal grandfather.

Johann Ambrosius Bach (1645–1695)
Another town piper and also a court musician, residing in Eisenach. He was the father, and his second wife Elisabeth Lämmerhirt (1644–1694) the mother, of

JOHANN SEBASTIAN BACH (March 21, 1685 to July 28, 1750)

The nomenclature of the Bach family has always been confusing, due to their maddening propensity for using the same names over and over. While at first they seemed content to have only two names per individual, they early developed the practice of using three. That the first name was often Johann only added a further complexity. Nowadays members of the family are generally identified by their middle names, as Sebastian Bach, or by their initials as, C. P. E. (for Carl Philipp Emanuel) Bach.

This once almost innumerable family, a veritable network of musicians, died out in the last century. In 1843, when a memorial to Bach sponsored by Felix Mendelssohn was erected in Leipzig, only one male member of the family could be found—Wilhelm Friedrich Ernst Bach (1759–1845), a minor composer, who was the son of Johann Christoph Friedrich, the only married son of Sebastian and Anna Magdalena Bach. Wilhelm Friedrich Ernst thus became the sole representative of the clan at the dedication ceremony.

Altogether, Johann Sebastian Bach had twenty children, seventeen grandchildren, fourteen great-grandchildren, and one great-great-grandchild. The last survivor was a great-granddaughter, Carolina Augusta Wilhelmine, daughter of Wilhelm Friedrich Ernst. She died on May 13, 1871. Thus the great Bach line ended.

The Hungarian Connection

Q.   Was Bach a Hungarian?
A.   No, but he thought he was.

ach is so automatically depicted as the epitome of German composers that it is startling to learn that he himself was under the impression that he was of Hungarian stock.

The question of the family's national origin goes back to Veit Bach, described as a baker or miller, said to have been born in the little town of Wechmar, near Gotha in Thuringia, southwest of Berlin. Early in his life Veit Bach traveled to Hungary and settled down there, setting up shop as a "white bread baker," playing his zither for recreation, and eventually returning to Wechmar because the religious climate in Hungary was hostile to Protestantism.

That, at least, is the conclusion of many modern scholars.

However, in Bach's own day the prevalent opinion seems to have been that the family started in Hungary. Johann Sebastian Bach himself knew that Veit had come to Wechmar from Hungary, but was unaware that he had started from the same town in the first place. Accordingly, Bach believed that he was descended from Hungarian stock. This belief is reflected in a brief biography of Bach published in 1732 in J. G. Walther's *Musical Lexicon*, presumably with the knowledge of Bach himself. Reports the *Lexicon:* "The Bach family is said to have originated in Hungary, and all those who have borne this name, so far as is known, are said to have devoted themselves to music."

In fact, some modern scholars incline to the belief that Veit Bach may actually have been born not in Wechmar, but somewhere in the Austro-Hungarian empire of the Hapsburgs, and moved to Germany only when persecutions of non-Catholics began. They also point out that the designation "Hungary" might actually mean Slovakia or Moravia, and say that there is evidence pointing to the town of Pressburg (now Bratislava in modern Czechoslovakia) as a birthplace for Veit. The entire controversy would seem to support Pablo Casals' remark that Bach "is among those geniuses who·shine over all nations and all times."

The Other Sebastians

ave you ever heard of Johann Sebastiani, composer of the *Passion According to St. Matthew*? In one of music's more curious coincidences, a composer of that name flourished in Germany from 1622 to 1683, dying two years before the birth of Johann Sebastian Bach. What is more, among his most notable works was a *Passion According to St. Matthew*, composed in 1672, over 50 years before the Bach *Passion*. It even displayed some of the same musical devices Bach was later to employ in his work, such as the inclusion of devotional chorales and the use of a rich string sound to accompany the utterances of Jesus.

Sebastiani, born near Weimar in 1622, studied for a time in Italy, which may be where he picked up the Italianate version of his name. He died in Königsberg in East Prussia (now Kaliningrad, in the Soviet Union), where he was in the service of the elector of Brandenburg (another Bach coincidence when one remembers that the name is attached to the Brandenburg concertos!). He also composed other religious works and a set of funeral songs.

Did Johann Sebastian know of Johann Sebastiani? It's an intriguing question to which, alas, no answer is available.

In Bach's own family, the name Sebastian was fairly unusual. No one had borne it before him; he received it in honor of a family friend, Sebastian Nagel, a musician who was one of his two godfathers (the other was named Johann Georg Koch). Two of Bach's grandchildren were named for him, but one, born to his daughter Elisabeth Juliana Friderica, lived only two weeks. Bach's son Carl Philipp Emanuel named one of his children Johann Sebastian Bach. This Johann Sebastian—who for some reason preferred to call himself Johann Samuel—became not a musician but a painter, achieving a modest reputation and moving to Rome, where he died at the age of 30.

The closest that music has come since to someone of the same name was John Sebastian, the harmonica virtuoso, who died in 1980.

Postwar Music

ach was born a generation after the conclusion of the Thirty Years War—the most devastating conflict ever to hit Germany, barring, of course, those of our own times. The war, which lasted from 1618 to 1648, involved most of the western European countries—France, Sweden, Spain, Austria, Italy, Denmark, and the various German states—and was instigated by religious disputes as well as by political rivalries. The battles had a particularly ruinous effect on German territories, on which most of them were fought. The population of Germany was reduced from 20,000,000 to 13,500,000; whole cities such as Magdeburg were razed; the land was ruined.

Bach, of course, would have heard stories of those terrible

times. One sometimes wonders whether a work like his Cantata No. 25, with its tenor recitative opening with the words, "The whole world is only a hospital," and its pervasive elegiac tone, may not be a reflection of that era.

By Bach's birth, however, Germany had made considerable strides toward recovery. Every effort was made to repopulate the country. Taxes were placed upon unmarried women; at the Congress of Franconia, held in 1650 at Nuremberg, a resolution was adopted permitting husbands to take two wives (a program soon abandoned). By 1700 the population was back to 20,000,000, the cities had been rebuilt, and commercial centers like Leipzig and Frankfurt were reinvigorated by their trade fairs.

In the arts, too, the war's repressive effects began to abate. Music had been pretty much driven from the courts of princes busily engaged in fighting, but had continued in liturgical settings and also in the homes and farms of ordinary folk, where singing and dancing provided touches of recreation and repose amid the horrors of destruction.

With the signing of the Peace of Westphalia at Münster in 1648, music underwent a renascence in princely and ducal halls, as well as in cities and towns. The Holy Roman Empire had been, by this time, greatly weakened and decentralized so that there now were more than 300 practically independent "states" in Germany, each with its own ruler, military, currency—and musical establishment. Sixty-three of these were ruled by clerics, fifty-one were "free cities," and most of the others were governed by minor royalty.

For petty princes as well as for grander ones the maintenance of a court "orchestra," no matter how tiny, was considered a requisite. Pay was scanty and musicians were treated as servants, but the opportunity to survive by playing music was certainly there. Bach's father Ambrosius was a violinist in the musical establishment of the Duke of Eisenach, and Bach himself was to earn his living in several princely establishments, including those of Weimar and Cöthen.

Musical composition proliferated in the last half of the seventeenth century in Germany, along with musical performance. The demarcation between composing and performing then was much less marked than it is now; many of the great church organists of the time also were composers, and capellmeisters played their own music as well as that of others.

Many composers seized upon the popular dance forms that had not died out during the war era and that now began to flourish even more vigorously at local gatherings such as street and commercial fairs—wherever popular entertainment was to be found. German town musicians—"town pipers," they were usually called—played these dance tunes with enthusiasm; in fact, they are credited with having given the pieces the name *partie*, or *partita*—meaning a complete whole made up of many parts. Dances were adapted from all countries, as indicated by their names—allemande (Germany), gigue (England), sarabande (Spain), courante (France). Their appeal reached beyond the town pipers to the serious composers who flourished in the late years of the seventeenth century, and adapted them to instrumental suites capable of reflecting a wide expressive and emotional range. Johann Sebastian Bach wrote partitas and suites for many instruments, including clavier, violin, cello, lute, and full orchestra, touching them all with his genius.

What Else Was New

hile 1685 was a bright year for music, it was pretty dismal in most other respects. Its most notable political and sociological event was the Revocation of the Edict of Nantes by King Louis XIV of France, by which any exercise of the reformed religion was prohibited and the Roman Catholic faith imposed throughout the country, not to mention throughout France's considerable holdings in the New World. Under Louis's action, French Huguenots were not only deprived of their religion, they were forbidden to emigrate. Nevertheless, thousands managed to flee France for haven in other lands, including some of the German states. The Revocation produced tremendous turmoil and tension in France, and played its part in the gradual buildup of grievances that led to the French Revolution.

England, too, was beset with political and religious strife, with King James II trying to win freedom of worship for his Catholic co-religionists as opposed to the supremacy of the Anglican Church. James was dethroned in 1686, to be succeeded by William and Mary. King George I of the House of Hanover mounted the throne in 1714.

Overseas in the American colonies William Penn had just entered into a treaty with the Indians and laid out the city of Philadelphia (1683), while in 1686 a Dominion of New England was formed through consolidation of the New England colonies. In 1706 the Salem witchcraft trials were held. Throughout the colonies, and especially in the northeast, attempts at greater local political control were on the rise, and the seeds of discontent began to grow that eventually would lead to the American Revolution, a quarter of a century after the death of Bach.

In Germany, Frederick the Great was born in 1712 and became King of Prussia in 1740. He was probably the only great historical personage of the day who had the slightest idea of Johann Sebastian Bach's existence, and certainly the only one to extend to him an invitation to come visit.

Bach's Lost Childhood

 ach's childhood is "lost" in the sense that very little is known about it. He left no memoir of his early days; there are no contemporary reports; and his school records are scanty.

But his childhood was lost in a more literal sense because both of his parents died—less than a year apart, of unspecified illnesses—when he was a child. He was raised from the age of 10 on by his brother Johann Christoph Bach, 14 years older.

Bach's father, Ambrosius Bach, was a violinist, so the presumption is that it was he who taught his young son to play the violin and gave him other music instruction, but no one knows this to be a fact. Bach's mother, Elisabeth Lämmerhirt, was the daughter of a furrier. In her years with

Ambrosius she bore six sons and two daughters; three of the sons survived, Johann Sebastian being the youngest. Elisabeth died in 1694, and seven months later Ambrosius remarried—only to die himself within three months.

Eisenach, where Bach was born 37 years after the end of the Thirty Years War, was a town of some importance in Thuringia. It lay in a beautiful forested countryside. The house of Bach's birth is still standing and is open to visitors. Its address is Frauenplan, 21, and its appearance cannot have changed very much in 300 years. It's a large, three-story structure, with the ground level originally used as a hay barn and stable. The Bach family lived on the two upper floors, and from the windows Bach could see the ancient castle of Wartburg, atop a hill, where Martin Luther had been imprisoned for a time and where Richard Wagner two centuries later was to lay the scene of the singing contest in his opera *Tannhäuser*.

Today the house, which has belonged since 1907 to the Neue Bach Gesellschaft, is a museum with period furnishings, although not the Bach family's own. There also is a fine collection of musical instruments, including two owned by Bach, a viola da gamba and a viola pomposa, which he invented (see Bach's Instruments). Eisenach itself lies within the German Democratic Republic (East Germany), as do the other sites principally associated with Bach's life—Leipzig, Ohrdruf, Arnstadt, Mühlhausen, Cöthen, and Weimar. Within a few miles of Weimar is the site of the Nazis' Buchenwald concentration camp.

Compulsory education began to be instituted in much of Germany after the Thirty Years War, and Bach started school in Eisenach at around age 8. Schooling then consisted of what might be called the Four Rs—reading, writing, arithmetic, and religion. Much of the reading was in Latin. History was mainly biblical history, with no attention to local or national events—an unfortunate omission, since the annals of Thuringia were studded with intriguing names of rulers such as Henry the Fowler, Louis the Bearded, Louis the Springer, Louis the Hard, Albert the Degenerate, Frederick the Undaunted, Frederick the Grave, Frederick the Strong, and John Frederick the Magnanimous.

After his parents' death, Christoph Bach, who was 24 and had recently married Dorothea von Hof, and become a church organist in Ohrdruf, 30 miles away, took his two younger brothers to live with him in his new household. The local lyceum was on the next block and Sebastian was forthwith enrolled and continued there for five years. Some of his school records survive and they show him hovering near the top of his classes, though he never was singled out as a budding genius.

Music, specifically religious music, was part of the curriculum and Sebastian also received instruction from his brother. When Christoph denied him the use of a volume of organ pieces by several well-known living composers on the grounds that they were too difficult for him, Sebastian sneaked downstairs and copied them out by moonlight over a period of time—only to have Christoph take away his copy when he discovered what he'd done.

While Bach never lacked for shelter, food, warmth, and musical instruction, his childhood was hardly passed in carefree circumstances. He must have been delighted when, at the age of 15, his brother, who by now had three small children of his own in his crowded house, decided to enroll him at the prestigious choir school of St. Michael's in Lüneburg, 150 miles away in Saxony. The year was 1700, and after two years of schooling and training at Lüneburg Bach was ready to start looking for a job.

Bach's Job Résumé

ach was an inveterate job hunter. Even when he had a good job, as he did most of his life, he was always looking for a better one. Following is a list of the positions he actually held, and the searches that went on in between.

1. St. Michael's Church School at Lüneburg (1700–1702). Bach's first paying job helped put him through school. He was a boy soprano in the choir, and after his voice broke at about age 16 he assumed some accompanying and administrative duties. At Lüneburg he received free upkeep and education and earned the equivalent of around $25 a year. (For comparative purposes, it may be noted that the deacon of the church was paid around $100 a year. It should also

be remembered that money went much further in those days than in these).*

After completing his studies at Lüneburg Bach went into the job market and auditioned for an organist's position at Sängerhausen, about 50 miles from his native city of Eisenach. He won the competition, but the local ruler turned him down in favor of another applicant, a personal favorite. Undaunted, Bach quickly found other employment.

2. Violinist in a court orchestra at Weimar (1703). This is an early indication of Bach's skill as a string player—sometimes overlooked in his celebrity as an organist.

Bach seems to have regarded the Weimar post, which was in a rather minor orchestra, as a temporary stopping-off place while he waited for a job as an organist; in any case, he remained there only six months.

3. Organist at the New Church in Arnstadt (1703–1707). Bach got this job after being asked to test and evaluate a new organ that had been installed. He played it so well that, at the age of 18, he was engaged as organist and choir director. His pay was 50 florins (about $150) a year, plus $175 for board and lodging. He lived at an establishment called the Golden Crown Inn.

---

*An attempt has been made to translate German currency values of Bach's time into modern U.S. currency, but such figures can only be rough approximations. Those used in this book are based largely on equivalents used by Will and Ariel Durant in *The Age of Voltaire* (1965), adjusted for 1985.

Bach had been eager to obtain the post at Arnstadt, but throughout his four years there he kept his eyes open for another job. While there he rejected a job at Lübeck because he didn't want to marry the daughter of its current occupant, Dietrich Buxtehude (see Bach in Love). His employers complained that he overstayed his time-off allowance on his Lübeck trip; they also objected to his organ playing as too fancy. So when he tried out for, and secured, another job, they probably sighed with relief.

4. Organist at St. Blasius's Church, Mühlhausen (1707–1708). The church authorities offered him the same salary he had been getting at Arnstadt, plus "54 bushels of grain, 2 cords of wood, and 3 pounds of fish" delivered to the door annually; they also paid his moving expenses. Perhaps their most important contribution was to pay for the publication of his church motet "God Is My King" (No. 71). It was the first time Bach ever saw any of his music in print.

For reasons not clear, Bach didn't get along particularly well with his new employers and parishioners and quarreling broke out. However, his leavetaking after less than a year was surprisingly amicable. Bach wrote a letter explaining that he'd been offered a better job and wished to be released, and the parish authorities acquiesced, asking only that he continue to monitor an organ reconstruction project he had initiated——which he did.

5. Chamber musician and court organist to Duke Wilhelm Ernst at Weimar (1708–1717). This job raised Bach's pay to about $400 (156 gulden) a year, with annual increments. As "konzertmeister" he was second-in-command to the "capellmeister," wearing a court uniform on state occasions. His previous Weimar post had been in a smaller orchestra; now

BACH'S JOB RÉSUMÉ

Weimar, where Bach worked for 9 years and wound up
in jail for 6 weeks.

he had a leading role as organist, violinist, and harpsichordist,
as well as a composer whose merit was being noticed (the
Toccata and Fugue in D minor dates from this period, as
does "Jesu, Joy of Man's Desiring"). He was called regularly
to other cities to evaluate the organs there.

*Bach's restlessness set in at Weimar no less than elsewhere. In-
specting a new organ in the city of Halle, Bach opened talks with
the authorities about moving there but finally decided to stay put.
However, when the old capellmeister at Weimar died, Bach expected
to replace him in the No. 1 position. When the duke passed over him
and named an incompetent in his stead, Bach accepted an offer to
join the establishment of Prince Leopold of Anhalt-Cöthen. The duke*

was enraged and resisted Bach's departure for six weeks (see Bach in Jail).

6. Capellmeister of Cöthen (1717–1723). Bach was in charge of virtually all the music at Prince Leopold of Anhalt-Cöthen's establishment. It was here that he really flowered as a secular composer, producing such masterpieces as the Brandenburg concertos and the *Goldberg Variations*, although he continued to compose religious music as well. He was well-paid, with a salary of over $800, and lived with his family in a wing of the duke's castle. It was the best job he had ever had, and he might have stayed on indefinitely had it not been for the death of the prince's wife, who loved music. The prince remarried, and the new princess turned out to be a woman who cared little—and spent less—for music.

Even at Cöthen Bach kept his eye on the eighteenth-century equivalent of the want ads. During a visit to Hamburg he played for a near-legendary organist named Johann Adam Reinken, then 97 years old, who told him: "I thought this art was dead, but I see it lives on in you." As long as he was there, Bach applied for Reinken's job, but it went to another organist, J. J. Heitmann, who allegedly paid a bribe to get it. It's possible that Bach asked for the Hamburg job more from force of habit than any real desire; it was not until the musical climate at Cöthen underwent a change that he began seriously to look elsewhere.

7. Cantor of St. Thomas's Church and School, music director of the city of Leipzig (1723–1750). Although Bach held this position for more than a quarter of a century and wrote many of his greatest religious works during this period, his life in Leipzig, a city of 30,000, was almost a constant battle with the authorities. He was not their first choice; they

would have preferred either Georg Philipp Telemann or Christoph Graupner, but both were unavailable. The town's chief councillor, a gentleman named Dr. Platz, achieved immortality of a sort for philosophically remarking that since they couldn't get "the best man," they would have to take a "mediocrity"—meaning Bach.

During his years in Leipzig Bach wrote and directed an average of ten church cantatas annually, composed the *St. Matthew Passion* and the *B minor Mass*, and produced the secular music for his Zimmermann's Coffee House concerts. He also had to teach music and, for some years, Latin to schoolboys; file disciplinary reports on the students; perform many administrative duties. The result was a never-ending series of disputes and squabbles with the school and church authorities which at times surely made him wonder why he had ever left Cöthen. His Leipzig income, however, was substantial for the time, amounting to around 700 thalers ($1,400) a year, plus rent-free living quarters. When he died, his estate was valued at between $2,000 and $3,000.

In 1730, seven years after coming to Leipzig, Bach wrote a heartfelt letter to an old schoolmate and friend, Georg Erdmann, who by then had become a lawyer and diplomat and was stationed in Danzig. Bach wrote that he had made a mistake in changing "my position of Capellmeister [in Cöthen] for that of Cantor [in Leipzig]." Then he went on to detail the frustrations and vexations of his job and, finally, appealed: "Should Your Honor know of or find a suitable post in your city for an old and faithful servant, I beg you most humbly to put in a most gracious word of recommendation for me. . . ."

One hopes that Erdmann did put in a good word somewhere for his old friend, but whether he did or didn't, it made no difference. Bach remained in Leipzig for the rest of his life, complaining about his job, and creating masterpieces to the end.

Bach in Love

hen Bach was 21 years old and working as organist at the New Church in Arnstadt, he was reprimanded by the Church Consistory for "making music" with "a stranger maiden" in the choir loft. Girls at that time were not permitted to sing in German church choirs (boy sopranos and altos were employed in their place), so the music making of Bach and his lady friend must have been of a private nature indeed.

Bach's early biographers have assumed that the young woman in question was Bach's young second cousin Maria Barbara Bach, whom he married the following year. However, no documentary evidence exists as to the "stranger maiden's" identity, and about all the incident proves is that as a young man Bach had interests other than the purely musical.

In fact, when Bach had to make a choice between musical advancement and personal affection he opted for the latter. In 1705, at the age of 20, he decided to journey to Lübeck, 50 miles away, to hear the famous organist Dietrich Buxtehude, many years his senior. Tradition says that he walked all the way. Buxtehude had gotten his job at Lübeck, a prestigious post, by marrying the daughter of the previous organist there. Buxtehude, too, had a daughter, and being ready to retire, was offering her hand to whoever succeeded him. She must have been singularly ill-favored, for two other aspiring young organists, Johann Mattheson and George Frideric Handel, had turned down both the job and the girl.

Apparently the same offer was made to Bach, with the same results. Although Lübeck would have been a giant stride for him professionally, he returned to Arnstadt where two years later he married Maria Barbara. Their union produced seven children, of whom four survived infancy.

Maria Barbara could trace her ancestry back to Hans Bach, so presumably she was not ignorant of music. She married at age 23 and died at 36. Her death, totally unexpected, occurred while Bach was on a musical assignment in Carlsbad with his employer at the time, Prince Leopold of Anhalt-Cöthen.

Seventeen months later, Bach, then 37, married Anna Magdalena Wülcken, 20, daughter of a court trumpeter and herself a young singer of ability. If his first marriage had been a success, his second was sheer perfection, for Johann Sebastian and Anna Magdalena were deeply attached to each other and remained so to the end of his life. She bore him thirteen children, of whom six survived childhood. Bach commissioned an artist to do her portrait—surely a sign of his affection—but it has disappeared.

Unfortunately, her stepchildren, especially Carl Philipp

Emanuel, appear to have regarded her with resentment and hostility; after Sebastian Bach's death they appropriated most of his assets and left her nearly destitute.

Not only did Anna Magdalena play a leading part in Bach's home musicales, she also worked with her husband as a copyist, transcribing many of his works, and was able to play much of his keyboard music. Bach compiled for her two books of his works, a keyboard practice booklet, much of which has been lost, and a volume entitled *The Little Musical Notebook for Anna Magdalena Bach*—more commonly known as the *Anna Magdalena Book*—as charming and touching a gift as a musician has ever given to his wife.

The *Anna Magdalena Book*, embossed in gold and with gilt edges and copied out by Anna Magdalena herself, is filled with delightful pieces such as dances, marches, and songs— even the theme of the *Goldberg Variations*. Among the songs is the beautiful little love song "*Bist du bei mir*," obviously addressed to his wife:

> If you are with me
> I go with joy
> To death and my rest.
> Ah, how happy
> Would be my end
> If your beautiful hands
> Would close my faithful eyes.

It was the last service Anna Magdalena was to perform for him after 28 years of marriage. She herself lived another 10 years and died in a poorhouse.

Bach's Opus 1

ach, of course, never used opus numbers him-
self—they were a characteristic of the classical rather than
the baroque era—and we have no reliable information on
any pieces he may have written during his school years or
directly after.

About the first Bach work that can be accurately dated
also happens to be one of the most unusual in the entire
canon—a piece of frankly programmatic music for which the
composer, then 19, provided a written scenario. Its title is
Capriccio sopra la lontananza del suo fratello dilettissimo—Capriccio
on the Departure of a Beloved Brother.

When Sebastian Bach, at the age of 10, went to live with
his oldest brother Johann Christoph in Ohrdruf, along with

him went the middle brother of the family, 13-year-old Johann Jakob. However, Johann Jakob appears not to have remained very long in Ohrdruf, but to have returned to his native town Eisenach, where he succeeded his late father as a town musician, his instrument being the oboe. Jakob was one Bach who liked to move around, and after Eisenach he wandered as far east as Poland in several musical jobs.

In 1704, at the age of 22, Jakob enlisted in the Swedish Guard as an oboe player. Sweden then was one of the European powers, under the leadership of Charles XII, and the Guard was its elite corps. Before beginning his enlistment he returned to Ohrdruf for a final visit to family and friends. Johann Sebastian cherished the warm familial feelings that were common to the entire clan and to salute his older brother he composed this Capriccio, presumably designed to be played on the clavichord.

The Capriccio has six sections, each with a title given by Bach:

1. Persuasion by his friends to talk him out of his journey.

2. Depiction of the various calamities that might befall him in foreign parts.

3. A general lamentation by the friends. (Apparently their efforts in Parts 1 and 2 have been unavailing!)

4. The friends, seeing it cannot be otherwise, come to take their leave. (The coach must be waiting, since Bach gives them only eleven bars!)

5. *Aria di Postiglione*—the coachman's song, which is punctuated by the sound of the post horns.

6. A double fugue on the postilion's horn call. This is

the most elaborate section and undoubtedly was meant to express Bach's own sorrows upon the departure of his brother. Throughout his life it was for the fugue that he reserved some of his most powerful and personal utterances and in this early piece he was already showing his deep involvement with this particular musical form.

Johann Jakob Bach, incidentally, lived the dashing life he wanted under Charles XII. He went with him to the Battle of Poltava in 1709, where the Swedes suffered a Napoleonic-scale defeat during an attempted invasion of Russia, and later followed the king on a campaign in Turkey. He took flute lessons in Constantinople from a famous player named Pierre Gabriel Buffardin and then, in 1713, left the military service to retire to Stockholm as a court musician. He must have remained in touch with Sebastian, for both their names appear in some legal documents regarding a small legacy in 1720, but the two do not seem to have ever actually met again. He died in Stockholm in 1722 at the age of 40, and one hopes that he remembered to the end the musical farewell with which his younger brother had sent him off on a life of adventure.

Two Wives and
Twenty Children

 hile a few of the great composers (Vivaldi and Mozart among them) are about as prolific as Bach in musical output, none has ever approached him in the number of children they brought into the world. By his two wives Bach was the father of twenty children over a 34-year period. Only ten survived childhood, but of those who did, four became well-known composers, their fame in their own day surpassing their father's. The following are Bach's children by each of his wives, in the order of their appearance.

Maria Barbara (Bach) Bach
(1684 –1720)

Catharina Dorothea (1708–1774).

Bach's first child, a daughter born after the family's move from Mühlhausen to Weimar, never married.

Wilhelm Friedemann (1710–1784).

Known as the "Halle Bach" because he became organist in that city. Friedemann benefited greatly from his father's instruction and became an excellent organist and a skilled composer. Since Bach wanted his sons to have the university education that he himself had lacked, he also enrolled Wilhelm Friedemann, as well as Carl Philipp Emanuel and Johann Christoph Friedrich subsequently, at the University of Leipzig as law students. However, Wilhelm Friedemann, despite his musical gifts, late in his life gave way to discontent and dissipation. He drifted from one musical job to the other and died poor and unemployed.

Maria Sophia and Johann Christoph (1713–1713).

These twin children died shortly after their birth. Twins were not unprecedented in the Bach family. Johann Sebastian's father, Johann Ambrosius, had had a twin brother who was said to be his exact image in appearance and in temperament. Both were violinists and played in a similar style; they suffered from the same illnesses, and died within a few months of each other.

Carl Philipp Emanuel (1714–1788).

The "Berlin" or "Hamburg Bach," he was an important figure in the musical life of both cities. In Berlin he was court musician to Frederick the Great, in Hamburg he succeeded Georg Philipp Telemann as musical director of that city's principal churches. His *Essay on the True Art of Playing Keyboard Instruments* was an important treatise and very influential in its time. C. P. E. Bach (sometimes designated K. P. E., following the German spelling of his first name) was probably the most productive composer of Sebastian's sons, with some of his music still performed.

Johann Gottfried Bernhard (1715–1739).

For a short time he became organist at Mühlhausen, a post held by his father 28 years previously, but he decided to study law instead. He died at 24.

Leopold August (1718–1719).

Anna Magdalena (Wülcken) Bach (1701–1760)

Christiana Sophie Henriette (1723–1726).

Gottfried Heinrich (1724–1763).

To the grief borne by Bach over the early death of so many of his children was added the sorrow caused by the fact that Gottfried Heinrich, the oldest son of his second marriage, was a half-wit. Heinrich, according to Philipp Emanuel Bach, had great musical instincts that never developed. Heinrich lived to the age of 39.

Christian Gottlieb (1725–1728).

Elisabeth Juliana Friderica (1726–1759).

The only one of Bach's daughters to marry. (See Bach's Son-in-Law.)

Ernst Andreas (1727–1727).

Regine Johanna (1728–1733).

Christiana Benedicta (1730–1730).

Christiana Dorothea (1731–1732).

Johann Christoph Friedrich (1732–1795).
The "Bückeburg Bach" was court chamber musician at Bückeburg, a small city near Hanover. Less brilliant than his brothers, he was nevertheless a solid musician. Among his compositions was a cantata entitled *Die Amerikanerin*.

Johann August Abraham (1733–1733).

Johann Christian (1735–1782).
Known as the "London" or "Milan Bach," Johann Christian made the greatest impact on the international scene of all of Bach's sons. He also was the only one to abandon Lutheranism and convert to Catholicism. For 2 years he was organist at Milan Cathedral, but he moved to England to become music master to the wife of King George III, as well as a popular musician on the London scene. A prolific if facile composer, he was a leader in the changeover from the baroque to the classical style, being particularly admired by the young Wolfgang Amadeus Mozart. Johann Christian once quipped that he "composed to live," whereas his brother Carl Philipp Emanuel "lived to compose."

Johanna Carolina (1737–1781).

Regine Susanna (1742–1809).
The last of Bach's children to die. Like her mother, Anna Magdalena, she passed her last days in poverty. In 1801 Johann Friedrich Rochlitz, director of the

Leipzig Gewandhaus concerts, launched a public appeal for funds for Regine Susanna Bach. Among the first to offer help was Ludwig van Beethoven. He volunteered to raise money for her quickly, before "this brook has dried up and we can no longer supply it with water."*

*A play on Bach's name. See Bach's Puntheon.

Bach's Son-in-Law

ach's sons are famous, but what about his son-in-law? His name was Johann Christoph Altnikol, and both as a human being and a composer he deserves more than the cursory—or less—notice that he usually gets.

Altnikol (1720–1759) was a native of Silesia who came to Leipzig to study theology at the University. He also was an excellent organist and had a good bass voice, and it wasn't long before he became Bach's student and later his assistant.

Altnikol developed a great affection for the cantor, and even more for the cantor's daughter Elisabeth, then 23 years old. The two were married in January 1749; it was the only wedding that ever took place in Bach's house, and he and his wife made the most of it.

Bach, who was never averse to helping out a family member, did all he could to further Altnikol's career; when the Town Council of the city of Naumburg told him that they needed an organist he forthwith suggested Altnikol—without the latter's knowledge. Altnikol got the job, largely on Bach's recommendation that he could not only play the organ but was also "exceptionally skilled in composition, in singing and on the violin."

Among his other attributes Altnikol was a skilled copyist and of great assistance to Bach in this capacity. Bach fell ill soon after the marriage took place, and it was to Altnikol that he dictated his last work, a chorale prelude. Its original title was "When We Are in Deepest Need," but Bach changed this to "Before Thy Throne with This I Come." Altnikol also was among the small group at Bach's bedside when he died. He and his wife named their first child, born October 4, 1749, Johann Sebastian; unfortunately the boy lived only two weeks. Altnikol performed one more service for his father-in-law: after Bach's death he took his half-witted son, Heinrich, into his home.

Bach and Handel

 eldom have two composers begun their lives in such similar circumstances, and then taken such divergent paths, as Johann Sebastian Bach and George Frideric Handel. They were born less than a month apart at a distance of 80 miles from one another: Handel, February 23, 1685, at Halle in Saxony; Bach, March 21, 1685, in Eisenach in Thuringia. Bach's father was a musician, Handel's a barber turned surgeon. Both were well trained in music and became excellent organists.

Handel attended Halle University for a while but left because he wished to compose and to travel. He began writing operas at the age of 19, went to Italy for 4 years, and then to England, where he anglicized his name from Georg Friederich Händel and eventually became a British subject. Unlike Bach, Handel was an inveterate bachelor; domesticity held no charms for him. He preferred to spend his life upon the world stage as a composer, producer, and promoter of operas and later oratorios. In striking contrast to Bach, he loved being a personage of international importance, and was very conscious of the likelihood that his music would live on after him. One anecdote that has survived tells of the Prince of Wales, the future King George III, expressing his pleasure after listening to Handel play his music. "A good boy, a good boy," Handel cried out, "you shall protect my fame when I am dead."

Bach and Handel were well aware of each other's existence if only because of each other's early fame as organ virtuosos. However, they never actually met—through no fault of Bach's. On at least two occasions after he had become famous in England and throughout Europe, Handel returned to Halle during business trips to the continent to recruit singers. On both occasions Bach tried to arrange a meeting with a fellow musician whom he obviously respected highly.

In 1719, Bach, who was then at Cöthen, walked 20 miles to Halle with the intention of calling on Handel, whom he had heard was there, only to find that he had departed earlier that same day. Ten years later, he tried again. Being temporarily ill, he sent his son Wilhelm Friedemann, then 19, to Halle with a courteous invitation to Handel to visit Bach in Leipzig. But Handel, for whatever reason, was unable to come. One Handel biographer, Percy M. Young, comments: "To be truthful, it looks as though Handel was lacking in enthusiasm. He was a busy man, he probably reasoned, and provincial organists had a habit of tedious severity in conversation unpalatable to the traveled and worldly-wise."

BACH AND HANDEL

It seems highly unlikely that Handel knew any of Bach's music, or that he would have felt much interest in it if he had. Bach, however, was acquainted with Handel's, possibly to a considerable extent. When he was cantor at Leipzig he and Anna Magdalena together copied out the score of a Passion setting by Handel, evidently for use at a church service there. Twenty-three pages are in Bach's handwriting, thirty-seven in Anna Magdalena's.

Personally acquainted or not, the two great composers have gone through musical history linked together, each embodying in his own way the culmination of the baroque. Today Handel's operas are undergoing a revival much as are Bach's cantatas, and knowledge of the achievements of both men is deepening. The enduring fame of each is assured. And yet there seems little question that it is Bach's music that remains supremely stimulating to musical minds today, as it has to great musicians of former years.

Perhaps the most telling comment is that of Johannes Brahms, as reported by Albert Schweitzer in his Bach biography. Brahms awaited with impatience each volume of the Bach Gesellschaft—the collected edition of his works—as it appeared, and the moment he received it dropped everything else he was doing to go through it. "For," he said, "with old Bach there are always surprises and I always learn something new." When a new volume of the new edition of Handel's works arrived, he would put it on the shelf saying: "It ought to be very interesting. I will go through it as soon as I have the time."

The Third Man

he year 1685 was music's greatest vintage year. Not only Handel and Bach were born that year, but so was the Italian keyboard composer and virtuoso Domenico Scarlatti, who wrote over 600 sonatas and other works for harpsichord, besides operas, cantatas, and sacred music. Scarlatti, who was born in Rome on October 26, 1685, was the son of the celebrated opera composer Alessandro Scarlatti, and, like Handel, an international personality. He died in Madrid in 1757—seven years after Bach and two before Handel.

Scarlatti and Bach never met each other, and there is no evidence that either knew of the other's music—although Bach may have seen some Scarlatti scores, since his knowledge of Italian music was considerable. However, Scarlatti and

Handel were acquainted with one another. They met in Rome in 1709 and engaged in a friendly keyboard competition, in which they were adjudged to be about equal on the harpsichord, but with Handel clearly the superior organist. The two men remained on a friendly footing; Handel had a liking for Scarlatti's operas, which were sometimes given in the same London theater as his own.

Like Handel, Scarlatti hobnobbed with royalty. At various times he served as maestro di cappella to the Queen of Poland and at the Vatican. He was also court cembalist to the King of Portugal and, according to some accounts, performed in London and Dublin.

Scarlatti spent much of his life in Spain, where he was appointed "maestro de cámara" to Queen Maria Barbara. In Spain he left off writing operas and concentrated on harpsichord sonatas, exerting great influence over the course of Spanish keyboard music over succeeding generations. So great was his keyboard virtuosity that he is regarded almost as the father of modern piano playing.

The closest that music has come to producing such an exceptional vintage crop of composers was 1813, when both Richard Wagner and Giuseppe Verdi were born. Like the two great figures of the baroque, Bach and Handel, these two operatic masters of the nineteenth century never met.

Bach in Jail

 ach is the only great composer known to have undergone arrest by the authorities. His crime? Trying to quit a job he didn't like.

The incident, which occurred when Bach was 32, casts a curious light upon legal practices and class distinctions of the early eighteenth century, not to mention the social repute—or lack of it—in which paid musicians were held by the aristocracy. In 1717 Bach gave notice to his employer, Duke Wilhelm Ernst of Weimar, whom he had served for nearly 10 years, explaining that he had received a better offer from the Prince of Anhalt-Cöthen, with higher pay and work more to his liking.

When Bach informed the duke of his intention to leave,

the ruler forthwith placed Bach under arrest. Some commentators have endeavored to minimize the duke's action by concluding that the confinement was merely a form of house arrest and that Bach simply remained at home while the duke simmered down. However, this is nowhere indicated; in fact the ducal court's official report clearly states that "the quondam concertmaster and organist Bach was confined to the County Judge's place of detention for too stubbornly forcing the issue of his dismissal."

Bach's sentence lasted from November 6 to December 2, after which he was freed with a notice of "unfavorable discharge." Wherever it actually took place, Bach's forcible incarceration seems an act of aristocratic callousness and meanness of spirit that ranks with the kick in the pants with which Mozart received his dismissal from the Archbishop of Salzburg 60 years later.

Bach at the Table

 assure you that I can already form a concert, both vocal and instrumental, of my own family, particularly since my wife sings a very pure soprano and my eldest daughter joins in bravely."

Thus wrote Bach to his old friend Georg Erdmann in 1730, and it is pleasant to conjure up a picture of him, seated at the parlor harpsichord, leading his wife and children in an informal household recital.

But man does not live by music alone, and Bach also had other daily essentials on his mind, including food, drink, and comfort. As a family man, he was an excellent provider, obtaining the best housing, provisions, and luxuries that his income—reasonably adequate but never lavish—could sustain.

The quality of his lodgings varied. In Cöthen he and his

family lived in the duke's castle, with spacious surroundings and the palace grounds for the children to play in. In Leipzig they were housed in the St. Thomas's school building, an ancient and rather grim-looking edifice. Floor space was adequate, but the rooms were smallish and in close proximity to the student housing facilities. Life was bound to be crowded; the size of Bach's family almost guaranteed that it would be so.

Food was never in short supply. Bach's employment contracts at several of his posts included the delivery of certain provisions and firewood. He was a hearty eater, and he liked his wine. When a cask of good Rhenish, sent by a cousin, sprung a leak during shipment to his house, he mourned the loss of "so noble a gift of God" (see Sayings of J. S. Bach). However, he also was a thrifty man; he calculated that the shipping charges he would have to pay for another cask would amount to 5 groschen a quart—so he asked his cousin to please not send a replacement. Among other documents that have been preserved is a receipt signed by Bach in 1732 for taxes on three barrels of beer, which were apparently delivered to his door without any spillage.

Meals in Bach's time inclined to the heavy side, with soup, fish, and several varieties of poultry, game, or meat served at the same repast. If neither Bach nor his sons were slender, there were reasons.

Unfortunately, there is no Anna Magdalena Cookbook to go along with the Anna Magdalena Notebook, so we don't know much about the daily fare in the Bach household. However, the menu of a banquet Bach attended has been preserved. It was given by the church authorities at Halle on May 3, 1716, following his testing and approving of the organ there.

The menu shows both the quantity and variety of the

food served on a festive occasion. The size of the assembled company is not given, but meats listed include "Baffallemote" (apparently a Germanization of *boeuf à la mode*), smoked ham, mutton, and roast veal. For fish there was pike in butter sauce. Vegetables included potatoes, peas, mixed spinach and chickory, asparagus, lettuce, pumpkins, fritters, and radishes. Desserts specified are preserved lemon rind and preserved cherries. It's impossible to believe that some church councillor's wife didn't also send over a cake or two. What is certain is that nobody went away hungry.

The Pedagogical Bach

n a rare burst of indignation, Bach's nineteenth-century biographer Philipp Spitta remarks upon "the absurdity of employing a musician like Bach to teach a parcel of schoolboys."

But that is just what Bach spent a good portion of his life doing, and he was not very happy about it. Bach began his teaching career as a 20-year-old choir instructor while he was organist in Arnstadt. The teaching was only a subsidiary part of his job, not specifically described in his terms of employment, and the boys of the choir seem to have been a particularly unruly lot. After about a year relations between Bach and his "pupils" deteriorated to the point of physical violence.

One evening Bach was walking through the marketplace with a girl cousin when he was set upon by a young man named Geyersbach, who played the bassoon in the instrumental ensemble Bach directed in the church. Bach had curtly told him that he was a "nanny-goat bassoonist" (*Zippelfagottist* is the expressive German word) and Geyersbach now demanded an apology for the insult. Bach, whether for his own sake or his cousin's, desired to avoid a scene, and denied he had insulted Geyersbach personally. But Geyersbach insisted he had insulted his bassoon, which was the same thing. The two exchanged abuse until the student suddenly lashed out at Bach with a stick he was carrying. Bach, for some reason, was wearing a short sword at the time, and promptly drew it. However, other students intervened and separated them.

A hearing into the incident was held by the school authorities and both Bach and Geyersbach received reprimands. The authorities pointed out that Bach "already had the reputation of not getting along with the students" and that he should not have called Geyersbach a *Zippelfagottist*. "Man must live among the imperfect," they added by way of a philosophical summation.

After this unpromising start, it is no surprise to find that Bach's teaching career was a mixture of brilliant successes and depressing failures. The determining factor invariably was the quality of the student. Gifted musicians loved him and profited greatly from his counsel, but mediocre or incompetent musicians derived no benefit at all. As a matter of fact, he couldn't stand them. Part of his duties at Leipzig involved testing students seeking admission to the St. Thomas's School for their musical attainments. He would ruthlessly reject as many as half of a batch of twenty applicants, listing them simply as having "no musical accomplishments." Even some of the successful ones he accepted only grudgingly, with comments like "Gottfried Christoph Hoffmann, of Nebra, aged 16, has a passable alto voice, but his proficiency is still rather poor," or "The above-named Wünzer has a somewhat weak voice, and little proficiency as yet, but he should (if private practice is diligently maintained) become usable in time." Part of Bach's agreement with the Thomas School required him to teach five lessons a week of classroom Latin himself or to provide a substitute teacher; he tried doing it for a time but soon gave it up and paid a colleague named Petzold 50 thalers a year to replace him. There seems no doubt that the students weren't loath to bid him *Vale*.

Bach's most successful pupils undoubtedly were his own sons, so many of whom carved out successful careers as composers or organists. He was particularly productive in teaching the art of keyboard playing, whether clavier or organ. Bach took private pupils, and usually set them to studying his Two- or Three-Part Inventions (how many students afterwards were to work on these same pieces!) and his *Well-Tempered Clavier*. One student, Heinrich Nikolaus Gerber, tells how Bach, after listening to the student play, would then play his own pieces himself. When that happened, comments Gerber, "the hours seemed to be but minutes."

Although Bach possessed perhaps the most profound musical mind of any composer who ever lived, his teaching, whether of keyboard or composition, tended to avoid the theoretical and to concentrate upon the practical. His son Carl Philipp Emanuel commented that he "omitted all the *dry species* of counterpoint that are given in Fux* and oth-

*Johann Joseph Fux (1660–1741). Austrian composer and theorist. The italics in the passage are C. P. E. Bach's.

ers. . . . As for the invention of ideas, he required this from the very beginning, and anyone who had none he advised to stay away from composition altogether."

Toward the end of his life Bach was invited to join a newly formed Society for Musical Science in Leipzig, and he accepted the honor. Probably the invitation was extended because Bach was known to be of such great musical learning, yet, according to a fellow member, Johann Mattheson, he never expressed much interest in any possible connection between music and mathematics. One of the first notices published after his death said flatly: "Bach never went into a deep theoretical study of music." Yet everything he composed attested his mastery of musical theory and science; his knowledge was not to be conveyed in abstract form but through playing and listening to his music. He himself seemed to understand this perfectly, as when, on the title page of his *Little Organ Book*, he wrote:

In Praise of the Almighty's Will
And for my Neighbor's Greater Skill.

Bach Versus Ernesti

ll the frustrations and vexations experienced by Bach at St. Thomas's crystallized in 1736 into a 2-year-long running dispute with Johann August Ernesti, the school's new rector. Bach was nearly 50, Ernesti 27, with a brilliant scholastic record already behind him. Besides being young, Ernesti was ambitious and "modern" in outlook, eager to expand the school's curriculum in the direction of greater relevance and practicality. To make things worse, he didn't care for music. To him it was a necessary evil—the school's traditions insisted upon it—but it also was a distraction from what he regarded as genuine learning and scholarly pursuits. "Do you want to be a beer-hall fiddler?" he would sneeringly ask students who he thought spent too much time practicing.

Bach, with his insistence on the school's traditional values and curriculum, was soon engaged in a bitter battle with Ernesti. It broke out when the rector expelled a student who was serving as Bach's prefect, or assistant, and appointed another in his place. Bach regarded this action as an infringement on his function and chased the new prefect out of the rehearsal room with "great shouting and noise." Subsequent battles broke out at the school's supper table, where Bach ate with the boys, and even in the choir gallery, in full hearing of the congregation during Sunday services. The boys were caught in the middle ground between contradictory commands from cantor and rector.

Bach and Ernesti also carried on the war by writing long letters detailing their charges and complaints to the Town Council. Bach would begin his documents with a long and flowery salutation and then get down to particulars. On August 19, 1736, he wrote as follows:

"To their Magnificences, Most Noble, Distinguished, Steadfast and Learned, also Most Wise Gentlemen, the Burgomasters and Members of the Most Worshipful Municipal Government of the Town of Leipzig, My Most Honored Masters and Patrons. . . . You most graciously will still remember, Your Magnificences and Noble Sirs, what I was forced to report to Your Honors concerning the *disordres* (*sic*) that were caused eight days ago during the public divine service by the actions of the Rector of the Thomas School. . . . Since the same thing took place today, both in the morning and in the afternoon, to avoid a commotion in the Church and a *turbatio sacrorum* I decided to conduct the motet myself. . . . The situation is becoming worse and worse, so that without the most vigorous intervention on the part of You, My High Patrons, I will hardly be able to maintain my position with the students you have entrusted to me. . . ."

BACH VERSUS ERNESTI

Bach also appealed to the elector of Saxony, Friedrich Augustus II, but in truth neither the elector nor the Town Council seemed eager to intervene in this prickly quarrel between two strong-minded individuals. Eventually the elector gave Bach an honorary title of Court Composer that strengthened his hand somewhat (see Bach Among the Aristocrats). The quarrel with Ernesti never was settled by any formal decree or decision. Things quieted down, and the two disputants coexisted because they had no other choice. But to the end of Bach's life—Ernesti remained rector until 1759—both men regarded each other with hostility and suspicion. Their quarrel, in a way, was one more chapter in the eternal battle between the practical and the creative minds. Ernesti's antagonism should have been no surprise to Bach: there's an Ernesti in every artist's life.

The Great Organ Competition

hile few of Bach's musical compatriots realized his stature as a composer, virtually all were aware of his excellence as an organist. So when the most famous organist of France, Louis Marchand, came to Dresden on a visit in 1717, it was only natural that someone should stage a keyboard competition between him and Bach.

The contest apparently was suggested by another Frenchman, J. B. Volumier, concertmaster in Dresden, who was either jealous of Marchand or held a grudge against him. Bach, who then was organist and chamber musician at Weimar, eagerly accepted the idea and journeyed to Dresden.

Marchand was no mean competitor. He was organist to King Louis XV of France, had had several volumes of com-

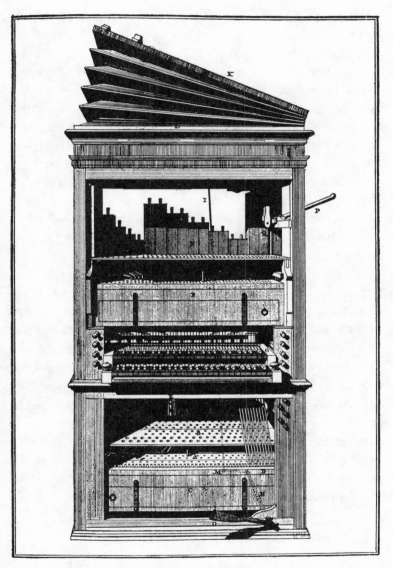

Details of the construction of an eighteenth-century organ. Bach frequently was called upon to test and evaluate such instruments.

positions published, and was particularly admired for his elegant style. Naturally, interest among the music lovers at the Dresden court ran high.

It's not clear just what form the contest was to take—sight-reading, extemporizing, developing variations—or even whether the organ, the harpsichord, or both were to be the weapons of the duel. If Bach had not had complete confidence in his ability to win he acquired it soon after his arrival; for Volumier, the Frenchman who had sponsored the contest, sneaked him in to hear his rival play at a practice session. In fact, according to one witness, it was only *after* Bach heard Marchand play that he actually dispatched a courteous challenge. Marchand, with equal courtesy, accepted, and a date was set.

Came the appointed time, and a "large company of persons of high rank and both sexes" gathered at the palace of Count Flemming, minister of state, where the competition was to take place. Bach was there, the count was there, the onlookers were there—but no Marchand! After a long wait, they sent round to his lodgings, only to be informed that M. Marchand had suddenly remembered a pressing engagement elsewhere and left Dresden by the early morning fast coach. So Bach won the competition by default, and played a solo concert for his admirers. The best explanation of the surprising turn of events seems to be that Marchand, like Bach, had sneaked in to hear his rival practice, and again—like Bach—realized what the outcome would be.

Bach's Instruments

 ach was proficient upon so many instruments that he almost seems like an eighteenth-century one-man band. He was one of the greatest organists who ever lived, and an outstanding performer upon the clavichord, harpsichord, and Silbermann "fortepiano," a forerunner of the modern pianoforte. He also was an expert violinist, good enough to play in several court orchestras. According to his first biographer Forkel, he liked especially to play the viola in quartets, so he could sit, "as it were, in the middle of the harmony, whence he could best hear it and enjoy it, on both sides." Mozart, a generation later, is said to have preferred to occupy the same chair when playing quartets. Bach also played the cello and it is generally assumed that he could handle the lute, the guitar, and perhaps other plucked string instruments as well.

Bach also invented an instrument called the viola pomposa, between a viola and a cello in size, with five strings, for which, according to his biographer Spitta, he wrote a Suite in D Major, subsequently included among his six cello suites. The viola pomposa, whose strings were tuned C,G,D,A,E, was held on the arm and in front of the chest with the aid of a ribbon. Some doubt has been cast by modern scholars on Bach's connection with the viola pomposa, but early authorities are emphatic in stating that he laid out its specifications. In any case, this midget cello fell into disuse within a generation.

While few details have been recorded about Bach's skill as a string player, his keyboard technique was a never-ceasing source of astonishment to his contemporaries. He could play the organ better with his feet than others could with their hands, according to an obituary notice published soon after his death. Dr. Charles Burney, the English musical historian and traveler, reports that Bach "was so fond of full harmony that, besides a constant and active use of the pedals, he is said to have put down such keys by a stick in his mouth, as neither hands nor feet could reach." Someone must have been imposing upon the good doctor's credulity, but his picture of Bach adding to his organ tones with a stick between his teeth has a certain charm nevertheless.

Among home keyboard instruments Bach, according to Spitta, preferred the clavichord to the harpsichord, although he certainly was at ease on both. Six were among his possessions when he died, as opposed to two harpsichords. He also owned three violins, including one by a celebrated Austrian violin maker, Jakob Stainer; three violas; two cellos; one viola da gamba; and assorted other instruments.

Bach's contribution to the art of keyboard playing—

A viola da gamba player. The name means "leg viol."

keyboard in this case meaning the "clavier," a term that encompasses both clavichord and harpsichord—seems to have been enormous. He made far more use of the thumb than most of his predecessors, and he insisted that the fingers be well curved when striking the keys. He could trill with his little finger as evenly as with the others. Johann Mattheson said that Bach "never entered into deep theoretical considerations about music, and was all the more efficient in performance." His playing was natural and flexible. Spitta observes: "He never wrote a clavier piece which did not serve as a healthy gymnastic for the fingers; but on the other hand, he never composed anything which fulfilled no end than that of an exercise."

The most comprehensive tribute to Bach's abilities as a musical executant comes from Johann Matthias Gesner, who in 1730 became rector of the St. Thomas's School—in other words, Bach's boss. Gesner reports almost with awe the dexterity with which Bach, "going one way with his hands, and another way with the utmost celerity with his feet," could make an organ perform marvels of harmony.

Then he gives a fascinating picture of Bach as a conductor, in an era before conductors really existed as such: "Could you only see him, how . . . by presiding over thirty or forty performers all at once, recalling this one by a nod, another by a stamp of the foot, another with a warning finger, keeping time and tune; and while high tones are given out by some, deep tones by others, and notes between them by still others, this one man, standing alone in the midst of the loud sounds, having the hardest task of all, can discern at every moment if anyone goes astray, and can keep all the musicians in order, restore any waverer to certainty and preserve him from going wrong; rhythm is in his every limb, he takes in all the harmonies by his subtle ear, as if it were uttering all the different parts through the medium of his own mouth."

For all his adeptness with instruments, Bach never used them while composing—not even the clavier. "It was never his habit in composing to ask advice of his clavier," is the quaint way an early biographer named Ernst Ludwig Gerber puts it. He composed in his head, then wrote down what he heard in his mind on paper—and without making too many changes once he did so. Moreover, Forkel says that Bach could never understand why anyone should do otherwise. Composers who did their work not in their minds but at their instrument he dismissed contemptuously in one phrase: *Clavier-Ritter*, "Knights of the Keyboard."

Bach as a Plagiarist

n Act I of Giuseppe Verdi's opera *Falstaff*, the fat knight remarks to Bardolph and Pistol: "Art resides in this maxim: Steal with politeness and at the right time." His observation refers to their musical no less than their professional activities, for the scoundrelly pair have just mangled the tempo of a canon.

Verdi, of course, would never have dreamed of applying the same sentiment to Bach, a composer for whom he had considerable respect. Nevertheless, it accurately describes Bach's lifelong procedure of appropriating the music of other composers and adapting it to his own uses.

Copyright as we know it today did not exist in the eighteenth century in a legal sense; it may not even have existed as a philosophical concept. Some music (though not very much, considering the amount written) underwent publication and was available in printed form, but much of it existed only in manuscripts, which were copied out and circulated from hand to hand. A composer had no way of telling where his music might end up; what pay he received for it was invariably "up front."

Music was the center of Bach's life, and he never lost an opportunity to hear, perform, and study what was new. Unlike some of his leading contemporaries, including Handel, he never traveled to Italy. But he brought Italy to himself in the form of its music. Italian composers, especially Antonio Vivaldi, the "Red Priest" of Venice (so-called because of the color of his hair), fascinated him. Vivaldi, who lived from 1678 to 1741, poured out music by the ream, and much of it reached Bach in Leipzig. Particularly impressive were Vivaldi's violin concertos and—either because of the inherent interest of the music or because he needed material for his concerts at Zimmermann's—Bach rearranged them for clavier.

However he did not merely copy them; in his hands the music underwent subtle shifts and alterations. Vivaldi's scores were filled in, ornamented, given new flexibility and richness; they were not transcribed but transformed. The same treatment was given to other Italian composers that Bach admired—Alessandro Marcello, Antonio Lotti, Giuseppe Torelli. He similarly used music by German composers. He copied out some of Handel's music, apparently without actually adapting it.

But Bach's outside borrowings seem almost insignificant when compared to the extent with which he reused and recycled his own music. Especially in his vocal and choral music Bach's transformations and repetitions of material have kept scholars and musicologists busy for years. Secular cantatas were regularly turned into religious works. Religious works were reassembled and redistributed into new combinations. Thus the *Christmas*, *Easter*, and *Ascension Oratorios* all consist largely of music lifted from earlier cantatas. For some reason, musicologists call such works "parodies" rather than "plagiarisms"—an unfortunate choice in view of the common meaning of the word.

Sometimes there is similar transference of musical ideas between Bach's vocal and instrumental works. The Cantata No. 140, *"Wachet auf"* ("Sleepers, Awake"), contains in its fourth movement one of the most beautiful of all Bach's melodies, a soaring tenor line over an equally lovely, but completely different, violin accompaniment. Bach, who knew a good thing when he wrote it, promptly turned it into an organ piece, one of his six Schubler Chorales, named after the man who published them.

Even more striking, perhaps, is the way Bach turned a little sarabande he had composed for solo lute into the final chorus of the *St. Matthew Passion*, "Here by the Grave Sit We All Weeping." It may also be heard in a version for flute and continuo as part of the Partita in C minor. In these latter versions it is a lovely little piece that one can hardly imagine being expanded into a broad and spacious consolatory chorus.

Bach not only composed great music; he invariably developed it to its fullest potential. He makes plagiarism a respectable word.

Bach's Religion

 hen Bach came to Leipzig to assume the position
of cantor in 1723, his musical qualifications were considered
of no greater importance than his theological soundness. He
had to undergo a thorough examination as to his religious
beliefs, and it was only when he answered all questions as to
his doctrine satisfactorily that he was admitted to his new
post.

Leipzig was more than merely a good Lutheran town, it
was a veritable bastion of Protestantism. Sunday worship at
St. Thomas's went on virtually all day—early matins followed
by a main service from 7 to 11 A.M., then a noontime service
followed by a two-hour afternoon vespers. The city's churches
were one of Leipzig's major industries.

A performance of church music in the early eighteenth century. The "conductor" uses rolled-up music sheets.

After Bach's experience as organist at Arnstadt and Mühlhausen, composing and performing religious music was nothing new to him. There were other attractions for him in Leipzig, though, such as the opportunity of enrolling his sons at the university so that they might have the advanced education he had missed, but the religious atmosphere of the city was surely one in which he expected to feel at home.

Bach remained an orthodox Lutheran throughout his life. As a young organist in Mühlhausen he encountered a new trend called Pietism, a relatively rigorous and more personal form of Lutheranism which, among other things, deemphasized the importance of music in the service. Bach sided with the traditionalists if for no other reason than that to him music was the deepest expression of religious faith.

From his early years as a composer, Bach often adopted the practice of heading his manuscripts with the words "Jesu, Juva"—"Jesus, help me"—and concluding them with the initials S. D. G.—"Soli Deo Gloria," "To God Alone the Glory." But the most convincing attestation to his belief is, simply, the enormous output of religious music he produced—two Passions (St. Matthew and St. John), three oratorios (Ascension, Christmas, and Easter), six motets, a magnificat, the Mass in B minor, nearly 200 church cantatas, 143 chorale preludes for organ and dozens of other works. He also wrote much church music that has been lost. In his Leipzig years he composed five sets of church cantatas for all the Sundays and holy days of the ecclesiastical year, a total of about 300. However, only around three-fifths of these are extant. Those lost, it is believed, may have been sold by his son, Wilhelm Friedemann, when he was in financial difficulties during his last years.

Bach's cantatas are the most imposing body of church

music ever produced by one composer. All but thirty or so were written at Leipzig. Bach took many of his texts from Christian Friedrich Henrici, a poet and satirist who used the pseudonym Picander, but he turned to other writers as well, particularly a woman, Mariane von Ziegler (see Bach and Women).

Bach's church cantatas cover services the whole year round; a church today could offer them every Sunday and holy day—indeed, at least one church, Holy Trinity Lutheran in New York, does just that. Their dates are clearly designated—"Sunday After Ascension Day," "Twenty-Seventh Sunday After Trinity" (the famous "*Wachet auf*"), "First Sunday in Advent," and the like. Their titles convey their general nature—"The Heavens Laugh, the Earth Rejoices!," "Lord Jesus Christ, True Man and God," "Jesus, My Joy," "I Will the Cross-staff Gladly Carry." Bach took most of his texts and inspirations from the New Testament, just as Handel, in such oratorios as *Israel in Egypt* and *Saul*, took his from the Old. For many of his late-nineteenth- and twentieth-century admirers, Bach has become known as "the Fifth Evangelist."

With such an outpouring of liturgical music to his credit, any questions of Bach's innate religiosity and love for the church might seem beyond all doubt. But over the last 40 or 50 years a revisionist school of scholars has grown up to argue that Bach was a church composer only some of the time, and then because it was part of his job; that both his background and much of his personal musical interest was thoroughly secular; and that to relate almost everything he composed to his religious faith is to gain only a partial and misleading picture of the man.

Among those holding this opinion was Friedrich Blume, an eminent German musicologist who lived from 1893 to 1975. Blume's viewpoint has been called "Marxist," which seems an extreme description, but it certainly is at odds with the traditional version. Blume argues that much of Bach's church music—including portions of the *Christmas* and *Easter Oratorios*—consists of reworkings of previously composed secular pieces; that he did much of his best work before he became cantor of Leipzig; that a considerable proportion of his true musical interests was represented by his activities as an organ and harpischord virtuoso, and as a conductor in Zimmermann's Coffee House and other public places in Leipzig.

Blume set forth his views in a book called *Two Centuries of Bach: An Account of Changing Taste*, published on the 200th anniversary of Bach's death in 1950, and also in an article entitled "Outlines of a New Picture of Bach," in the British publication *Music and Letters* for July 1963. He argues that "Bach the supreme cantor, the creative servant of the Word of God, the staunch Lutheran is a legend" which "will have to be buried along with all the other traditional and beloved romantic illusions."

Even Bach's production of some 300 church cantatas during his 27 years in Leipzig—an average of ten such works a year—fails to shake the arguments of Blume and others who share his view. They point out that recent scholarly redating of the cantatas has established that these cantatas were written, at a furious pace, during Bach's first few years at St. Thomas's and that afterward he turned principally to secular music and, indeed, reduced his total output drastically. Karl Geiringer, the author of one of the best modern biographies of Bach, observes that the *Mass in B minor*, a work that has elements of both Lutheran and Roman Catholic liturgy, "might well indicate a mellowing in the aged master's attitude, a deviation from belligerent Lutheran orthodoxy toward a more ecumenical attitude."

Bach's entire life span and artistic expression encompassed

both the sacred and the secular; indeed, judging by the way he interchanged their musical materials he may indeed have felt that the line between them was anything but impassable. The questions raised by a skeptical generation of musicologists do not destroy the image of Bach as a religious composer, but they give a fresh picture of him as a human being deeply involved in all aspects of the world around him, as well as of the world to come.

Bach and the Opera

he conditions of Bach's employment as cantor in Leipzig included a stipulation that he should "so arrange the church music that it shall not be too long, or of such a nature as to have an operatic character."

Bach operatic? It seems almost like a contradiction in terms, yet the Leipzig Town Council may have come surprisingly close to the mark. For, despite his later image, Bach knew opera, enjoyed it, and attended performances as frequently as he could. His first contact with it presumably came in Hamburg, which he visited as a young man and which was a thriving operatic center. His interest continued throughout his life. His son Carl Philipp Emanuel recalled that when his father visited him in Berlin, he took him on a tour of that city's new opera house.

While there, Bach displayed keen knowledge of a branch of musical science with which he is seldom associated— acoustics. "I showed him the new opera house," Philipp Emanuel told Forkel. "He detected at once its virtues and defects (that is, as regards the sound of music in it). . . . He looked at the ceiling, and forthwith announced that the architect had done something remarkable without planning to do so, and without anyone's realizing it: namely, that if someone went to one corner of the oblong-shaped hall and whispered a few words very softly against the wall, a person standing in the corner diagonally opposite, facing the wall, would hear quite distinctly what was said, and no one elsewhere in the room would hear anything. . . . This effect was brought about by the arches in the vaulted ceiling, which he saw at once."

Bach did most of his opera going during his Leipzig years. Leipzig itself had little opera, but Dresden, 60 miles away, had a splendid opera house and Bach traveled there fairly often. He would say to his oldest son, Wilhelm Friedemann, whom he usually took along, "Well, Friedemann, shall we go again to hear the lovely Dresden ditties?" Bach's early biographers, who repeat the remark, say it was made half-jokingly. But there seems no reason to doubt that Bach went to the opera because he enjoyed it. One specific occasion upon which he is known to have been present was the premiere of Johann Adolph Hasse's Italian opera *Cleofide* on September 13, 1731. Hasse's wife, Faustina Bordoni, who sang in *Cleofide*, was one of the most celebrated mezzo-sopranos of the day, and the opera was a huge success. The following afternoon Bach gave an organ recital in St. Sophie's Church, and the entire cast and orchestra of the opera turned out to hear him.

BACH AND THE OPERA

An operatic influence is discernible in a number of Bach's own works, including the *Passion According to St. Matthew* with its recitatives, arias, and choruses. Some of his Leipzig listeners were distressed by the *St. Matthew*; a little old lady is recorded as crying out at its first performance: "God save us, my children! It's just as if one were at an opera-comedy!" Several modern attempts have been made to present the *St. Matthew* as an opera, including one in San Francisco in 1973. Julius Rudel contemplated a staged production for the New York City Opera during his tenure there, but he left before he could accomplish it.

Bach composed about twenty secular cantatas to both German and Italian texts, and a number of these display the "operatic character" that so worried the Leipzig church and municipal authorities. One of his first efforts in this direction was made at Weimar in 1716, when Duke Wilhelm Ernst (the same nobleman who later put Bach in jail for daring to leave his employ) ordered an allegorical cantata to be given during a hunting festival on the occasion of his thirty-fifth birthday. Bach's cantata, based on the legend of Diana the Huntress, has ten numbers including a quartet, a duet, several arias, a chorus, and recitatives. Some of the music is of direct charm, some of complex polyphony. Bach later adapted several of its sections to church compositions, evidently seeing no great stylistic difference between the secular and the sacred.

Even more operatic in nature are three of Bach's secular works, the *Coffee Cantata*, the *Peasant Cantata*, and *Phoebus and Pan*. All of these had texts by Picander who otherwise supported himself as a petty official in the local post office and excise department. Picander was a friend of Bach's, and by writing the texts for the composer's Leipzig church cantatas, he served him much as Lorenzo da Ponte served Mozart—though admittedly with less literary distinction.

The *Coffee Cantata* apparently was Picander's idea; at least, he first wrote the narrative as a satire and Bach set it to music in 1732. Coffee was then a new and fashionable beverage in Europe, with coffee houses opening up in profusion, and people of all ranks drinking little else. In Picander's *Coffee Cantata*, a burgher of Leipzig named Schlendrian tries to cure his daughter Lieschen of following the fad, which he does by threatening that if she doesn't give up coffee she will never find a husband. Lieschen, however, spreads the word that she will only marry a suitor who will allow her "to make coffee as I like it." The final number, which has a bubbly flute accompaniment, reaches the conclusion that, just as cats will never stop chasing mice, so will young women never stop drinking coffee.

Bach's *Coffee Cantata* was a big hit in Leipzig, undoubtedly being performed at Zimmermann's Coffee House. A performance of "Schlendrian and His Daughter Lieschen" was presented in Frankfurt-am-Main in 1739; if this was indeed Bach's little cantata it would have represented one of the few instances of his music being performed outside of his own part of Germany.

The *Peasant Cantata* is an earthy depiction of country life with both the peasantry and aristocracy represented among the characters. It's written in a thoroughly popular style with plenty of dance tunes in both the vocal and the instrumental portions of the work—all in all, one of the most cheerful of Bach's compositions.

Of all these semi-operatic works by Bach, only one, *Phoebus and Pan*, bears the distinction of having been presented on the stage of the Metropolitan Opera House in New York.

BACH AND THE OPERA

The date was January 15, 1942, and the short work was given on a double bill with Rimsky-Korsakov's *Le Coq d'Or*. The conductor was Sir Thomas Beecham, making his Met debut on the occasion.

Bach composed *Phoebus and Pan* as a good-natured but pointed jab at his most persistent critic, Johann Adolph Scheibe, a Leipzig-born organist and writer who kept attacking him for the alleged complexity and difficulty of his music. In reply, Bach asked Picander to make a satirical text based on the Greek myth of the contest between Phoebus Apollo, the god of the lyre, and Marsyas (later Pan), the inventor of flute playing. In the original legend Apollo is victorious and, being told he can do what he wants with his defeated opponent, orders him lashed. In a later version of the story, as retold by Ovid, the penalty is inflicted not on the flute player but upon his chief supporter, King Midas. And instead of being flayed, Midas is punished for having displayed such poor musical judgment by having the ears of an ass clapped to his head.

Bach wrote this lively piece in 1731 for performance by his Collegium Musicum, the young musicians who played at Zimmermann's Coffee House. The audiences of the time had no difficulty in recognizing Scheibe as the wearer of the ass's ears.

In the Metropolitan Opera production, the work, which lasts just under 1 hour, was extended by ballet music drawn from Bach's French Suites Nos. 1 and 3 in an orchestration by Eugene Goossens. The cast included Stella Andreva, Anna Kaskas, Frederick Jagel, Arthur Carron, Emery Darcy, and John Brownlee.

It would be pleasant to report that this charming little work was a huge success at the Met, but unfortunately it wasn't. The critics disliked the stylized baroque production and complained about the singers' lack of proper vocal style for the music. In a typical review Oscar Thompson wrote in the *New York Sun*: "As an opera, *Phoebus and Pan* remained a secular cantata. . . . Though its airs maintained their freshness and animation they pleaded for smaller and simpler quarters." *Phoebus and Pan* was given three more times that season, and dropped from view. Bach awaits his operatic rebirth.

Bach and the Dance

ach, who never wrote a ballet in his life, is among the most frequently represented composers upon today's dance stage. This in itself isn't surprising, because so much of the music he wrote was in forms that originally had been dances, from gigues to sarabandes. There's even a waltz in his *Peasant Cantata*! Again in contrast with the austere image in which he is so often depicted, Bach was well acquainted with the dance both in its courtly and staged manifestations. Before he began his actual working career at the age of 18 in Arnstadt he traveled, among other places, to the town of Celle, where the duke of Lüneburg had built a beautiful little theater for opera and ballet. It's believed that, in order to get in, he played the violin in the orchestra for a few nights. In any case, he saw some of the latest examples of French dancing, a style imported by the duke. He also copied out some of the French harpsichord pieces he heard there, including a rondeau by Couperin.

While nineteenth-century romantic choreographers paid little attention to Bach's music, the moderns have taken it up enthusiastically. Well over 100 dance works exist to Bach scores, by both ballet and modern-dance choreographers. The phenomenon is international. Bronislava Nijinska, sister of the great dancer Nijinsky, choreographed *Étude*, a six-movement ballet, in 1931, for Paris; Michel Fokine's *Les Elements* was set to Bach's Suite in B minor in London in 1937; Serge Lifar's *Dramma per Musica* was a balletic version of the *Coffee Cantata* in Monte Carlo in 1946.

The European list continues with such works as Roland Petit's *Le Jeune Homme et la Mort*, set to the Passacaglia in C minor, which had been used earlier by Doris Humphrey; Edward Cranko's *Brandenburgs Nos. 2 & 4*; Maurice Béjart's *Actus Tragicus*, based on the cantata of the same title, and his *Notre Faust*, which makes use of nothing less than the *Mass in B minor*!

American choreographers have been even more productive. Humphrey's *Air for the G String* came out in 1929, her *Passacaglia in C Minor* in 1938, and her *Brandenburg Concerto No. 4* was completed after her death in 1958 by Ruth Currier. Other notable American choreographers who have worked with Bach's music include Ted Shawn, Charles Weidman, José Limon, Paul Taylor, Lar Lubovitch and John Neumeier, who in 1984 turned the *St. Matthew Passion* into a four-hour-long dance drama.

But the greatest dance works to the music of Bach have been created by the New York City Ballet under the incom-

A French dancer at the time of Louis XIV.

parable George Balanchine. It really wasn't until Balanchine came to the United States in the mid-1930s that he began choreographing Bach's music. *Concerto Barocco*, set to the Concerto for Two Violins in D minor in 1940, has remained a popular repertory work ever since. Balanchine was fond of quoting Ezra Pound's line "Music rots when it gets too far from the dance"; his feeling was that it takes great music to make great ballet, whether composers intended it for that purpose or not. During Balanchine's Stravinsky Festival of

1972 he choreographed that composer's Choral Variations on Bach's *"Von Himmel Hoch."*

But perhaps the most stunning Bach ballet ever choreographed—indeed one of the most stunning ballets ever created to *anybody's* music—is Jerome Robbins's *Goldberg Variations*, first given by the New York City Ballet on May 27, 1971.

As a musical composition, the *Goldberg Variations* is one of the most remarkable pieces Bach ever wrote. Among other distinctions, it brought him a handsome monetary reward. Bach composed it on commission from Count Hermann Carl von Kayserling, Russian ambassador to the Court of Dresden. Kayserling, an insomniac, employed a clavier player named Johann Gottleib Goldberg, and he frequently asked Goldberg to play him music during his sleepless nights. Kayserling commissioned Bach to compose a work that might provide him with some post-bedtime diversion. Bach's answer was the music known ever since as the *Goldberg Variations*. It must have done the trick, because in gratitude the count sent Bach a snuffbox which, upon opening, proved to contain not snuff, but 100 louis d'or ($1,250).

Although they are filled with life, variety, and beauty, these thirty variations have long had an undeserved reputation for austerity—perhaps because they last 1 hour and 20 minutes and are written for a single keyboard instrument. But Bach never regarded them as a heavy work; the climactic variation is a "quodlibet"—that is, a humorous composition based on a melange of two or more popular tunes. The songs that make up variation XXX start "I have been so long away from you, I'm here, I'm here, I'm here," and "Kale and turnips don't suit my digestion." Once the joyous, elaborate quodlibet ends Bach, in a masterstroke, brings back the quiet, gentle sarabande that forms the original theme of the work.

BACH AND THE DANCE

Robbins wasn't the first choreographer to attempt this complex piece; William Dollar's *Air and Variations* utilized about half the music in 1938—at that time, he said, he was afraid ballet audiences wouldn't stand for more.

But Robbins's *Goldberg Variations* makes no compromises. A lone pianist sits at the far left side of the stage and plays the entire work straight through, repeats included. Two dancers perform the opening sarabande, then gradually the other dancers enter in various combinations and patterns—gay, brilliant, humorous, acrobatic, romantic, somber. The climax is an ensemble of stateliness and grandeur which gradually dwindles, until only the original couple is left on stage as the sarabande is repeated, dying into silence.

Robbins's choreography parallels Bach's music with fidelity, but also with ingenuity and imagination. He almost makes its polyphony visible, as he mirrors its moods and intricacies. Robbins says he was impelled to choreograph the *Goldberg Variations* after hearing Rosalyn Tureck play them on the piano: "I felt it was a journey, a trip, that it took you in a tremendous arc through a whole cycle of life and then, as it were, back to the beginning." Much the same can be said of his ballet.

Other ballet companies seem content to leave the challenge of the *Goldberg Variations* pretty much to the New York City Ballet, but for them it has become a yearly repertory work. Not the least gratifying aspect of its success is that it has introduced thousands of listeners to one of Bach's fascinating and rewarding masterpieces.

Bach and Women

ost German women of Bach's time abided within the traditional bounds of Kirche, Küche, Kinder—church, kitchen, children. Women's emancipation was slower in coming to Germany than to France or England, although it began to stir in the late eighteenth century in fashionable intellectual salons in Berlin run by Rachel Varnhagen, Henrietta Herz, and Dorothea Mendelssohn, daughter of philosopher Moses Mendelssohn.

During Bach's lifetime in Leipzig women intellectuals or professionals were rare. Women did not attend the university or sing in church choirs or vocal societies; if they wanted to read or perform music they did so inside their homes—provided they had time.

BACH AND WOMEN

Yet despite the prevailing attitudes, Bach managed to meet several exceptional women during his lifetime, and gave every indication that he enjoyed their company and respected their achievements. He appreciated his wife Anna Magdalena's musical talents no less than her skills and fortitude as a homemaker and as a mother who saw seven of her children die. He praised her voice and he relied on her abilities as a musical copyist; it doesn't take much imagination to envision him trying out some of his musical ideas on her and respecting her artistic judgment.

In Cöthen he had the only experience of his life of being in the employ of a woman—or at least a woman who could exert a considerable influence upon her husband. Princess Friedericke Henriette of Berenburg married Prince Leopold of Anhalt-Cöthen, for whom Bach had been working happily for a number of years. The new princess may have been a cultivated person, but she was only 19, and she didn't care for Bach's music. Accordingly he decided to move on to Leipzig. As luck would have it, the princess became seriously ill and died soon after her marriage, but by that time Bach had made his commitment to Leipzig. Bach appears to have harbored no resentment against the lady; in a letter some years later he rather put more blame upon the prince, saying that his musical disposition "had grown somewhat lukewarm, while at the same time the new princess served as an amusement to him." Perhaps he was merely being chivalrous.

Most of the women with whom Bach was acquainted were associated with music—just as most of the men were. Instances of his having written music for performance by women (aside from his wife and oldest daughter, who sang at home) are rare, but it is possible that a noted soprano of the day named Christiane Pauline Kellner sang the part of

Diana the Huntress in a cantata Bach wrote for a festivity held in a ducal hunting lodge while he was in the employ of the duke of Weimar.

In Leipzig Bach became an admirer of the reigning Italian mezzo-soprano of the day, Faustina Bordoni. Bach was far from alone in his liking for her; a brilliant performer, she had concert engagements and offers everywhere. In London she engaged in a famous hair-pulling match onstage with her soprano rival Francesca Cuzzoni. She was married to Johann Adolph Hasse, who became the director or the Dresden Opera House, a beautiful establishment, where she sang for 20 years. Bach liked and admired both Hasse and Faustina, and they undoubtedly were among the attractions that drew him to the Dresden Opera so often. They also came to visit him and Anna Magdalena in Leipzig several times in what one imagines must have turned into exciting occasions in the Bach household.

With a voice and a presence such as Faustina offered, it seems entirely credible that Bach composed some music for her. The most likely candidate among the cantatas is considered to be No. 51, "Rejoice in the Lord in All Lands," composed in 1730, the year that Faustina married Hasse and came to Dresden. It would certainly suit her voice, being a brilliant and showy mezzo-soprano solo with a virtuoso trumpet obbligato.

Bach was a member of an informal circle of literary and intellectual figures gathered around Johann Christoph Gottsched, a poet, critic, and professor at the University of Leipzig. The connection came about when Gottsched's young wife began taking music lessons from Bach's favorite student, Krebs, who promptly invited Bach to hear her play and also to attend musicales at the Gottsched home. Gottsched's wife, Luise

Adelgunde Victorie, in addition to being an excellent clavier player, also became the author of several stage comedies and translated nine volumes of Addison and Steele's *The Spectator* into German. Bach must have spent some stimulating evenings in this talented and lively company.

But the most intriguing woman he knew in Leipzig was a poet named Christiane Mariane von Ziegler, 10 years his junior. They may have met at Gottsched's, or been introduced by a mutual friend named Maria Elisabeth Taubert; in any case, they became not only friends but working associates.

Ziegler, a native of Leipzig, was the daughter of a prominent family named Romanus, and married early. By the time she was 30, she had lost two husbands and several children, and launched a professional literary career, publishing two volumes of verse and one of letters. She came into Gottsched's circle and on his recommendation received the honorary title of "Imperial Poet Laureate" from the University of Wittenberg. She also twice won the annual poetry prize given out by a Leipzig literary association, the Deutsche Gesellschaft. Eventually she married a philosophy professor at the University of Frankfurt.

She and Bach must have hit it off well, for she was a regular attendant at his Zimmermann's Coffee House concerts, undoubtedly raising a few eyebrows by invading this predominantly masculine milieu. Her comments on the low pay scale of the musicians there (see Zimmermann's Coffee House) must have been made with Bach's knowledge and approval, and the two formed a working partnership that lasted for some time.

Bach was always in need of textual material for his cantatas, and Mariane undoubtedly was flattered at the idea of having her verses set to music by the city's leading composer.

Accordingly in the spring of 1725 she provided him with the texts of no fewer than nine cantatas, combining church hymns, biblical quotations (mostly from St. John), and strophic poetry. Bach performed these Ziegler cantatas as part of his regular Sunday services at St. Thomas's; it would be interesting to know whether the church authorities realized the texts were by a woman. As for Mariane, she was pleased enough with her work to include the cantata texts in a published volume of her verses.

Whether Bach had a hand in the shaping of Mariane Ziegler's librettos or merely took what she wrote and set them to music isn't known. But his association with her is one more indication of an attitude toward women well in advance of many of his contemporaries.

Bach Among the Aristocrats

ealing with the aristocracy was an integral part of life to a musician with any pretensions at all in early seventeenth-century Germany. At Arnstadt Bach worked for a count, at Weimar for a duke, at Cöthen for a prince. Only at Mühlhausen, which was a "Free Imperial City," and at Leipzig, where the Town Council did the hiring and supervising, were his immediate surroundings bourgeois rather than aristocratic.

Nevertheless, even at Leipzig, where he bore the title of Music Director of the City (which he always preferred to his alternate title, Cantor of St. Thomas's), Bach had his contacts with royalty. These took the form of providing music for various aristocratic events and celebrations, with Bach usually enlisting his Collegium Musicum—the musicians of Zim- mermann's Coffee House—as the performers. He was par- ticularly assiduous in providing celebratory music for Friedrich Augustus II, elector of Saxony, who was crowned King of Poland in 1734. When the new monarch came to Leipzig Bach turned out a cantata (No. 215) on three days' notice— understandably recycling music he had already used in other works. The gala for the king, which coincided with Leipzig's Michaelmas Fair, was a festive event, but it ended on a sad note. One of Bach's musicians, a trumpeter in his mid-sixties named Gottfried Reiche, died of a heart attack evidently brought on by his exertions at a great torchlight parade the night before. Almost the entire Thomasschule, led by Bach, turned out for his funeral.

Bach's musical attentions to Friedrich Augustus II were no accident. Bach may have been a hardworking burgher of Leipzig, but he also was an artist of great pride and at least normal ambition who sought recognition and had no objection to preferment, royal or otherwise. The Elector-King, who had his court in Dresden, was obviously in a position to grant Bach some of the status that had been denied to him by the Leipzig Town Council.

Bach accordingly set his sights on receiving from Augustus the title of Composer to the Royal Court Capelle. To further his campaign he sent to "His Royal Majesty in Poland and Serene Electoral Highness of Saxony" the score of nothing less than one of his most stupendous works, the *Mass in B minor*. Along with it went an obsequiously modest letter de- scribing the work as an "insignificant example of my skill in *Musique*"—and then proceeding to describe the "undeserved affront" and "annoyances" to which he was being subjected in Leipzig. Whether the monarch ever actually heard the

Bach at Cöthen.

"*Musique*" is not known, but he did eventually confer upon Bach the title he coveted, and henceforth the Town Council seems to have treated him with a little more respect. The greatest gainer of all, of course, was the world at large, which received the *B minor Mass*.

Royalty was even more directly responsible for another of Bach's masterpieces, the *Musical Offering*. By 1747, when Bach was 62 years old, his son Philipp Emanuel had for 7 years held the position of court musician and accompanist to Frederick the Great, King of Prussia, in Potsdam. Frederick, an accomplished flutist, found in music his chief recreation from warfare, and he had heard of Bach's prowess as an organist both from Philipp Emanuel and from Count Kayserling, the insomniac diplomat who had commissioned the *Goldberg Variations*. So an invitation was extended, and on Sunday, May 7, Bach, who took with him on the journey his oldest son, Wilhelm Friedemann, reached Potsdam.

As it happened, a state concert was scheduled that evening from seven to nine, with the king himself among the performers. But as he was about to begin a solo, Frederick was handed a note. With his flute still in hand, he turned to the assembled musicians and said excitedly: "Gentlemen, old Bach is here!"

The planned concert was immediately abandoned, and "old Bach," who had gone to Philipp Emanuel's lodgings, was sent for forthwith. He wasn't even given time to change into the customary black formal dress worn at court, but presented himself in his rather wrinkled traveling clothes. He apologized for his costume when he arrived, but the king told him he wanted to talk about music, not clothing. Frederick had a collection of seven keyboard instruments, including several of the new "fortepianos" developed by Gottfried Silbermann.

Bach was a friend of Silbermann's and had given him some advice in the design of his instruments. So it was with considerable interest that he accepted the king's invitation to try them all out.

On the following day Bach played the organ at the Church of the Holy Ghost in Potsdam, but in the evening he was again back at the royal chateau. This time the king, who evidently had been thinking about it all day, presented him with a musical theme—known ever since as the "Royal Subject"—and requested him to improvise upon it. The king himself played it at the keyboard, and Bach sat down and immediately improvised a three-part fugue upon it.

The "Royal Subject" apparently fascinated Bach, for when he returned to Leipzig he composed a set of thirteen polyphonic pieces based upon it, which he entitled the *Musical Offering*, including fugues, canons, and a magnificent six-part ricercar. This was an old designation for fugal-type music; Bach probably used it because the name formed an acrostic for "Regis Iussu Cantio Et Reliqua Canonica Arte Resoluta"— "Upon the King's Demand, the Theme and Additions Resolved in Canonic Style"—which he inscribed upon the dedication copy to Frederick. Bach loved wordplays like that, just as he loved occasionally putting little tricks and puzzles into his music. In the *Musical Offering* some of the canons— pieces in which one melodic voice imitates another—move backward, some progress upside down, and one is "perpetual" and may be played endlessly.

Frederick's reaction to this staggering musical gift is unknown; for all his talent, he may not have been musician enough to appreciate its intricacies. At least there is no record of any acknowledgment to Bach, let alone a gift. But Bach himself knew what he had accomplished; he had the *Musical*

Offering printed and referred to it affectionately as "my Prussian fugue."

The trip to Potsdam and Berlin had been important to him for another reason. It had given him the opportunity to make the acquaintance of his first grandchild, Emanuel's son Johann August, born a year and a half previously. One would like to think that when he returned to Leipzig he remembered Johann the little at least as fondly as Frederick the Great.

The Heart of
the Fugue

omebody once defined a fugue as "a musical composition in which the voices come in one by one while the audience goes out one by one." It is a description that undoubtedly would have startled Johann Sebastian Bach, the greatest master of the fugue that music has ever known.

Far from being archaic or austere, the fugue in his day was a relatively new form, a seventeenth-century descendant of the motet, madrigal, and ricercar. While its basic nature was the repetition of the same subject in an overlapping progression, in the hands of an imaginative composer it could undergo intense musical development and build to powerful climaxes. Bach used fugues as a teaching tool, but he never regarded them as academic or forbidding. To him the fugue, whose name is derived from the Latin word for "flight," could convey drama and majesty, as in his Passacaglia and Fugue in C minor and his Toccata and Fugue in D minor, or charm and piquancy as in his "Little" Fugue in G minor.

Bach enjoyed a fugue as other men enjoy a feast. According to his son Carl Philipp Emanuel, he would listen intently to fugues by other composers, muttering what ought to be happening next and predicting what turn the music would now take. When his surmises proved correct, and the music did what he had forecast, he would nudge Philipp Emanuel—or whoever else was standing near by—with satisfaction.

George Bernard Shaw, among others, realized the heartfelt quality of Bach's fugal music when he wrote in 1885 as a young music critic in London: "Sebastian Bach could express in fugue or canon all the emotions that have ever been worthily expressed in music. Some of his fugues will be prized for their tenderness and pathos when many a melting sonata and poignant symphonic poem will be shelved forever."

In 1748, two years before he died, Bach apparently decided to write one work that, perhaps more than any other, would represent a distillation of his musical thought. What he intended to call it isn't known, but it has come down to the present under the name of *The Art of the Fugue*. It is written on four open staffs, with absolutely no indication of the instruments Bach wished it to be played upon. (Recordings have been made for harpsichord, organ, string quartet, chamber ensemble, and full orchestra.)

Bach didn't live to finish this gigantic work, but he did complete eighteen separate fugues, calling each a "Contrapunctus," on the same theme or a variant. This was no pedantic exercise for him, for within the discipline of the contrapuntal form he let his fancy run free. He even included several astonishing "mirror" fugues—that is, with the separate voices presented first in their original form and then inverted as in a reflected image. In the final, unfinished fugue, No. 19, he incorporated his own name, the notes B-A-C-H. (In German usage, our note B is written as H, while our B-flat is written as B.) Apparently Bach died just as he was working out the fugue in his own name.

Ever since, composers have tried to achieve completions of the B-A-C-H fugue, and some have also written fugues of their own on the subject. Among those who have attempted fugues or other music on the notes B-A-C-H have been Bach's son Johann Christian Bach, his favorite St. Thomas's pupil Johann Ludwig Krebs, Ludwig van Beethoven, Robert Schumann, Franz Liszt, Ferruccio Busoni, Nikolai Rimsky-Korsakov, Vincent d'Indy, Arnold Schoenberg, Anton Webern, Humphrey Searle, Krzysztof Penderecki. . . . Is it too much to think that at this very moment still another composer, yet unknown, is accepting the challenge?

What Bach Read
and Wrote

ach may not have been an intellectual in the modern sense of the word, but neither was he a simple, narrow burgher concerned exclusively with music and making a living. He was a man of the world—although, by his own choice, he kept that world geographically small. He never attended the university, but he was a good student who far surpassed in learning William Shakespeare's "small Latin and less Greek."

Bach's Latin studies included Cicero and a life of Alexander the Great. In Leipzig he actually *taught* Latin, however reluctantly. It must be assumed he had some acquaintance with Italian—at least of musical Italian, for he used its phrases often enough—and that he had a working knowledge of

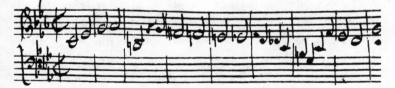

The theme of *The Musical Offering*, in Bach's writing.

French, perhaps speaking it a bit on his visit to Frederick the Great, where it was the court tongue. He chose to label his Brandenburg concertos, which he composed in Cöthen, *Six Concerts avec plusieurs instruments*—Six Concertos with Several Instruments—surely one of the great musical understatements of all time.

Like most of his educated contemporaries he was probably stronger on biblical and ancient history than on events of the middle ages. As for contemporary events in the neighboring German principalities, he would have kept up with them if only because of their possible effect upon his own fortunes.

Bach maintained an extensive library of books at his home, in addition to his musical collection. He died without making a will, but a list of his effects, down to his silver shoe buckles and one share he owned of Silesian mining stock, was made after his death by official curators appointed to the task. By the time they got there, however, Bach's two oldest sons, Friedemann and Emanuel, had removed all the music, books, and other material they wanted for themselves.

The list of Bach's books compiled by the curators consists almost exclusively of theological writings, a category obviously of no interest to the two sons. It is impossible to say whether Bach owned so many works on theology and religion because he was genuinely interested in them, because he felt they were becoming to his position as a religious school head-master, or because they had been given to him. He certainly would not have been the first book collector in history to have kept a volume or two on his shelf unread.

More than fifty titles are included in the reckoning, many of them tracts, pamphlets, and sermons. Luther was represented, of course, including a seven-volume set of his complete works. There were books relating to the struggles between the Pietists and the orthodox Lutherans. There was a pamphlet on "Atheism" which was valued in the estate at 4 groschen, and one on "Judaism," valued at 16. Bach also owned a biblical atlas and guide to ancient lands. The closest to a nonreligious book left behind by Bach's sons was Flavius Josephus's history *The Jewish War*, in German translation. The value of Bach's books altogether was put at 67 thalers, or around $135.

Such writings as we know of by Bach are principally official documents, many of them stemming from his frequent disputes with the Leipzig Town Council and school officials. He was exhaustive rather than eloquent in such documents, specifying his complaints in meticulous and sometimes re-petitive detail. Since he traveled so little he wrote few letters, a notable exception being his lengthy communication to his friend Georg Erdmann in 1731, detailing his dissatisfaction with conditions in Leipzig. Several of his letters are job rec-ommendations given to former pupils, and these, while couched in formal terms, achieve a certain personal warmth. He also developed a kind of homely flair in the little inscriptions with which he prefaced several works—"Composed for Music Lovers, to Refresh Their Spirits" on the title page of both his *Clavier-Übung* (Keyboard Practice) and *Goldberg Variations*, and "For the Use and Profit of Musical Youths Desirous of

Learning as well as for the Pastime of those Already Skilled in the Study" on *The Well-Tempered Clavier*.

Bach appears to have taken some hand in the preparation of the texts for some of his cantatas; he worked closely with Picander on the libretto of the *St. Matthew Passion*, a composition upon which he set great store. But his principal "literary" writing was done in the form of the verses he wrote for dedicatory purposes or for his own and his family's amusement. In Cöthen he wrote an elaborate dedication in rhyme to the newborn son of his patron, Prince Leopold, in which he incorporated his own signature into the rhyming scheme.

In the little books of his music he presented to his wife Anna Magdalena are several love songs he set to melodies taken from previously composed religious works, and he may have written some of these verses himself. Included in the second *Little Clavier Book for Anna Magdalena Bach* is a poem entitled "Edifying Thoughts of a Tobacco Smoker," of which Bach is believed to be the author:

> Whene'er I take my pipe and stuff it
> And smoke to pass the time away,
> My thoughts, as I sit there and puff it,
> Dwell on a picture sad and gray:
> It teaches me that very like
> Am I myself unto my pipe.

> Like me, this pipe so fragrant burning
> Is made of naught but earth and clay;
> To earth I too shall be returning.
> It falls and, ere I'd think to say,
> It breaks in two before my eyes;
> In store for me a like fate lies.

No stain the pipe's hue yet doth darken;
   It remains white. Thus do I know
That when to death's call I must harken
   My body, too, all pale will grow.
      To black beneath the sod 'twill turn,
      Likewise the pipe, if oft it burn.

Or when the pipe is fairly glowing,
   Behold then, instantaneously,
The smoke off into thin air going,
   Till naught but ash is left to see.
      Man's fame likewise away will burn
      And unto dust his body turn.

How oft it happens when one's smoking:
   The stopper's missing from its shelf,
And one goes with one's finger poking
   Into the bowl and burns oneself.
      If in the pipe such pain doth dwell,
      How hot must be the pains of Hell.

Thus o'er my pipe, in contemplation
   Of such things, I can constantly
Indulge in fruitful meditation,
   And so, puffing contentedly,
      On land, on sea, at home, abroad,
      I smoke my pipe and worship God.

It is as charming a self-portrait as any composer has left of himself in an hour of repose.

The Medical Bach

o live to the age of 65 in early seventeenth-century Europe was a substantial feat. Average life expectancy then was around 30, although it went higher if one survived infancy. Bach appears to have enjoyed good basic health and a robust constitution. Judging from his portraits, he was of middle height or taller, broad-shouldered, and somewhat corpulent. Beneath that wig, he may have been bald. The double chin seems to have been something of a family characteristic. Some modern physicians, studying the portraits, have found indications (such as a ruddy complexion) of high blood pressure, but this is sheer speculation.

It's possible that Bach did exhibit some signs of disease in his later years. A full year before he died, the Town Council of Leipzig held auditions "for the future occupancy of the post of Capellmeister upon the eventual occasion of the decease of Mr. Bach." They certainly wanted to be prepared!

But the only medical problem of Bach to be documented is his eye trouble. His vision apparently began to bother him in middle-life and became worse with the years. There is every indication that in his 60s—possibly earlier—he suffered from cataracts. His attempt to have them treated makes for sorry reading today.

The "physician" Bach chose was an itinerant oculist known as the Chevalier John Taylor, an Englishman who was the son of a female apothecary at Norwich. Taylor's training, if any, is obscure, but he apparently worked for a time in a London medical establishment and had invented a cataract needle and other instruments.

Taylor is said to have had a fashionable London practice but it must have dwindled, because he transferred his operations from England to the continent. He dressed in black, wore a flowing wig, and spoke a Latin syntax that bordered on gibberish. He wrote treatises and delivered lectures on ocular disease and obviously knew something about the eye; nevertheless, most modern medical authorities regard him as a quack.

Cataract surgery in Bach's day was called "couching," a method which had been in existence for at least 1,000 years. It consisted of jabbing a thick, sharply pointed needle into the eye, probing until the lens was found, and then pushing it downward into the vitreous jelly inside the eyeball. All this was done, of course, without anesthesia.

Describing the procedure in the *Annals of Ophthalmology* (January, 1974), Dr. Ramon Castroviejo writes: "These operations must have been a nightmare for patient and surgeon alike. The ordeal could only be accomplished with the participation of assistants to the surgeon whose only task was forcibly to keep the patient immobile and especially his head and eyelids. And the surgeon needed almost superhuman dexterity to carry out the procedures as rapidly as possible before the patient's lack of cooperation, readily understandable in view of the intense pain, ruined the outcome of the operation."

This, then, is the ordeal that Bach underwent in Leipzig around April 1, 1750, at the hands of Taylor—and not once but twice. The surgery was a total failure both times, which Taylor, with his customary glibness, ascribed to the patient's condition. "All circumstances (were) in his favor," he wrote, "motions of the pupil, light, etc. But upon drawing the curtain, we found the bottom defective from a paralytic disorder."

Not only did the operation fail to improve Bach's vision, it impaired his general health, with his entire system suffering. He spent his remaining months in his house, sitting in a darkened room, dictating music to Anna Magdalena and his son-in-law Altnikol. For a brief moment he thought his sight was returning, but this proved an illusion. In mid-July 1750 he suffered a stroke which was followed by a raging fever. Ten days later, on July 28, at about 8:45 P.M., he died, aged 65 years, 5 months, and 7 days.

Taylor, incidentally, continued his career unperturbed, eventually returning to London. In fact, in 1758 he operated on the eyes of George Frideric Handel, then 74 years old. The operation was as unsuccessful as that which he had performed on Bach, and Handel died the following year.

Bach's Burials

ach was buried in the St. Johann Cemetery in Leipzig. Apparently no tombstone was erected, and if there was any other marker it disappeared over the years. However, it was known that he had been buried in an oaken casket—one grade above the usual fir box—and a tradition persisted that the exact site was six paces south of the south tower of St. Johann's Church.

In 1894 excavations were undertaken during a rebuilding of the church, and it was decided to attempt to exhume Bach's body. Just six paces south of the tower, at the spot indicated, an oak coffin was found with the skeleton of an elderly man inside. A Professor Wilhelm His was called in to examine the remains, particularly the skull, and he announced that the body in the coffin was definitely that of Bach, the physical characteristics including prominent eyebrows, a prominent chin, and a somewhat protruding lower jaw. Working with a sculptor, Dr. His produced a three-dimensional cast of the head. Some scientists didn't put much stock in these 1894 proofs of authenticity; nevertheless, the supposed remains of Johann Sebastian Bach in 1950 were reinterred under a huge stone slab before the altar of the Thomaskirche, where he had worked and worshipped for a quarter of a century.

The reverence toward Bach displayed in 1894 and 1950 contrasts strikingly with the attitudes of the St. Thomas Church authorities at the time of Bach's death. A brief announcement that "the Esteemed and Highly Respected Mr. Johann Sebastian Bach" had "blissfully departed in God" was read from the pulpit, but no other memorial seems to have been contemplated either by church or town officials—no expression of regret, no motion of condolence, no plaque, tablet, or statue. In fact, something like a collective sigh of relief seems to have gone up. A successor, Gottlob Harrer, had already been designated, and he was formally installed forthwith. One Town Council member, Burgomaster Stieglitz, even seized the occasion to take a parting shot at Bach. Casting his vote for Harrer he said pointedly: "The School needs a Cantor and not a Capellmeister"—meaning, basically, that he wanted a choirleader, not a composer.

Thus St. Thomas's took leave of its greatest figure. But if the school authorities felt no great love for Bach, his disciples—the many young men who had learned to play the organ from him, benefited from his counsel, admired his compositions—kept his memory and music alive while most of the musical world ignored both. It's curious that of the

Bach in the last year of his life.

many young musicians Bach taught, none—if one excludes his own sons—became prominent composers, although many made their mark as organists all over Germany.

Perhaps one reason for this is that Bach's style of polyphonic composition was going out of style, to be swallowed up for a century and a half by the classical and romantic eras. Even his son Johann Christian referred to his father—we do not know whether in affection or derision—as "the old wig." Whatever kind of music they were writing themselves, Bach's disciples preserved the manuscripts of his own works that were at St. Thomas's, and purchased others from Anna Magdalena, who was in dire need of money after her husband's death.

Only some half-dozen works by Bach had actually seen publication, including the *Orgelbüchlein*, the *Clavier-Übung*, the *Musical Offering*, and *The Art of Fugue*—the latter engraved just after his death. The rest of his tremendous output was in manuscript form, and these were kept in the library of St. Thomas's by students and followers, who showed them to visiting musicians as they came through. Thanks largely to the efforts of the students the legacy of Bach was preserved, to await rediscovery.

Bach, Bismarck, and the Biographers

ohannes Brahms said that the two greatest events in German history during his lifetime were the founding of the German Empire by Bismarck and the complete publication of Bach by the Bach Gesellschaft.

Which was the greater of the two is a question that need not be answered here, but Brahms's remark is at least indicative of the place Bach has always held in many minds as a "German composer."

Curiously, Bach never referred to himself as a German, and such few of his writings as we have are refreshingly free of the least nationalistic or jingoistic allusion. Germany in his day was a conglomeration of petty states and fiefdoms, with no clear community of interests, as likely as not to be bickering with one another. The Holy Roman Empire was dying; only the rise of Prussia under Frederick II gave any indication of the nation that would eventually develop.

Bach saw relatively little of the area that was to become the German nation, scarcely straying far from Thuringia and Saxony. Had a national spirit been strong in his lifetime, he might have been caught up by it; as it was, he was content to spend his life speaking German and undoubtedly "thinking" German—but always with a purely local outlook. He never consciously wrote "German music," accepting his ideas from Italian, French, and possibly English musical sources as well as from his own countrymen. He was, to put it most simply, a "Bach," the inheritor of a proud family tradition.

But soon after his death, the Germanization of Bach began. By then German nationalism was beginning to rise—at the same time as an awareness of Bach's greatness as a composer was beginning to spread among his countrymen who had previously been largely unaware of it.

The first real attempt at a biography of Bach was made in 1802, when he had been dead half a century and the Napoleonic Wars had stirred the national consciousness of a dozen European countries. It was written by Johann Nikolaus Forkel, director of music at the University of Göttingen and was based in part on conversations with Bach's surviving sons. Forkel's title set the tone of his approach: *J. S. Bach's Life, Art and Works. For Patriotic Admirers of True Musical Art*. And while his book provides much valuable information, especially about Bach's life and personality, it sounds at times almost like a call to arms, as in its peroration: "And this man, the greatest musical poet and the greatest musical orator that ever existed, and probably ever will exist, was a German. Let his country be proud of him; let it be proud, but at the same time, be worthy of him!"

Much the same spirit infuses *the* great Bach biography,

the enormous three-volume work by Philipp Spitta published from 1873 to 1880, the decade immediately following the establishment of the Bismarckian Empire after the Franco-Prussian War. Spitta's all-inclusive, elegantly written book has remained the basic lode of Bach information for more than a century, despite various new factual discoveries and interpretive refinements. All Bach books written since, including this one, are based upon it. Yet it too resounds with the patriotic theme. Spitta found that Bach had a "thoroughly German spirit," that he "heartily and soberly enjoyed the pleasures of German family life," and that "it will not be possible that Bach should be forgotten so long as the German people exist." Spitta even advocated that the six suites Bach included in his *Clavier-Übung* be known as the "German Suites" as a counterbalance to his French and English Suites!

Most subsequent biographers have been less insistent upon the national aspects of Bach's art (see Bach and Schweitzer) and today he is regarded in as transcendent terms as Mozart or Beethoven. As for whether he regarded himself as a national hero or a universal genius, the best guess is that he never gave either possibility a thought.

Life After Bach

f Bach's music never completely disappeared from sight and from sound after his death, it was because of the efforts and interest of other musicians. This had been largely true even in his lifetime; aside possibly from the students who thronged Zimmermann's Coffee House in Leipzig the musical public at large never accorded him the warm response they gave his sons—or, for that matter, his great contemporary Handel. It has remained for the public of the twentieth century—more particularly of the latter half of that century—really to take Bach's music to heart.

But musicians, especially creative musicians, had only to come into contact with a few of his pieces to realize his significance. One of the first was Wolfgang Amadeus Mozart, who was born in 1756, six years after Bach's death. As an 8-year-old child prodigy Mozart was taken to London by his father, and there he met Bach's son, Johann Christian, the "English Bach," who at the age of 29 was a reigning favorite. Johann Christian was composing in a smoothly classical style quite unlike his father's, and he influenced young Mozart greatly.

Some 15 years later, when Mozart had settled in Vienna, he discovered the music of Johann Sebastian Bach at the home of Baron Gottfried van Swieten, an imperial court official and musical dilettante. Van Swieten knew of Bach's music and had organized a little chamber group to play it. Mozart was so delighted with it that he arranged several of Bach's fugues from *The Well-Tempered Clavier* for Van Swieten's string groups, and composed his own preludes for them. His wife Constanze encouraged him in this project; musicologist Alfred Einstein remarks, a bit cruelly, that this was "the only indication that she may have been really musical."

Even more impressive to Mozart was his first discovery of Bach's genius as a composer of polyphonic choral music. In 1789, two years before his death, Mozart set out with a pupil-friend, Prince Karl Lichnowsky, on a visit to Berlin. En route they stopped at Leipzig, where Mozart played Bach's old organ at St. Thomas's Church. The cantor then was Johann Friedrich Doles, who not only held Bach's old job since 1755 but had been among his pupils. Doles was so pleased that he had the St. Thomas Choir sing for Mozart one of Bach's eight-part motets, "Sing a New Song Unto the Lord."

According to an eyewitness, Friedrich Rochlitz, Mozart exclaimed: "Why, what is this? Now, *that* is something one can learn from!" He asked if there were any other motets and Doles, one of the Bach disciples who had eagerly guarded the manuscripts, quickly took them out. There were no full scores, only parts, but Mozart spread them all around him, "on his knees, on the floor, and on the chairs that were near him, and, forgetting everything else, did not get up again until he had looked through everything of Bach's that was there."

From that time forth a new complexity and sense of counterpoint becomes apparent in much of Mozart's music, observable in such works as his last opera *The Magic Flute*, his *Requiem*, and the finale of his Symphony No. 41 in C, the *Jupiter*, with its wonderful combination of the fugue and sonata forms.

Other Viennese-based composers also turned with interest to Bach's music. Joseph Haydn studied *The Well-Tempered Clavier*, the motets and the *B minor Mass*. Beethoven, like Mozart, played Bach fugues at Baron van Swieten's and deeply admired much of his other music, though his real preference may have been for Handel, a crusty bachelor after his own heart.

With the beginning of the nineteenth century, interest in Bach's music began slowly to permeate wider circles of music lovers. In 1801 three publishers, two in Germany and one in Switzerland, brought out editions of *The Well-Tempered Clavier*. Forkel published his biography in 1802 and it was translated into English. An article in the *Allgemeine Musikalische Zeitung* of Leipzig in 1801 likened Bach to Isaac Newton as one who "plumbed the depths of knowledge," and in 1818 the composer Carl Maria von Weber, one of the torch bearers of the romantic movement in German music, wrote an article in an encyclopedia saying that Bach had built "a true Gothic cathedral of art" and calling him "intrinsically Romantic and of true German basis, possibly in contrast to Handel's more antique greatness."

Thus the nineteenth century began—as does every era—to recreate Bach in its own image.

Bach and Mendelssohn

 lthough musicians like Haydn, Mozart, and Beethoven were aware of the existence and importance of Bach's music, to the public at large it remained virtually unknown. Such few pieces as were heard were likely to be performed during a church service. The public concert had come into being in Mozart's lifetime, and was a flourishing institution in Vienna, Paris, and London by Beethoven's day, but there was no place on the concert stage for the kind of music Bach had written.

But all that changed, literally overnight, on March 11, 1829, when Felix Mendelssohn conducted in Berlin the first performance in a century of Bach's *Passion According to St. Matthew*. In his own time, Mendelssohn was far more than a composer; he also was a pianist, a conductor, and a superb musical organizer of concerts, events, and festivals. He was only 20 at the time of his *St. Matthew* revival, but he had already composed the *Midsummer Night's Dream* overture and other works and was regarded as Europe's most brilliant young musician.

One of Mendelssohn's teachers had been Carl Friedrich Zelter, director of the Berlin Singakademie. Mendelssohn knew that a copy of Bach's *St. Matthew* score was under Zelter's care in the Academy's archives. One legend, popularized some years ago in a novel entitled *Beyond Desire* by Pierre La Mure, is that Zelter possessed the original manuscript and that it had been once used as wrapping paper by a cheesemonger. Actually Zelter's was only a copy, but complete and faithful. Mendelssohn studied it and, with the help of his friend the singer Eduard Devrient, determined to perform the work as a charity benefit in the hall of the Singakademie, exactly 100 years after its first performance, directed by Bach, at St. Thomas's in Leipzig. He assembled a total of 158 singers— 47 sopranos, 36 altos, 34 tenors, and 41 basses—and put in weeks of preparation with them.

Mendelssohn not only did the work of selecting, training, and rehearsing the singers and instrumentalists who were about to perform music they had never seen before; he also bore the expenses of the event. When the Singakademie authorities refused to waive the customary 50-thaler fee for the use of the hall, he dug down into his pockets and paid that, too. Most of the singers refused remuneration for performing; some even offered to pay their way in. Excitement about the concert spread through the city; the hall was sold out weeks in advance and more than a thousand people were turned away at the door.

The *St. Matthew Passion* takes 4 hours to perform, and Mendelssohn thus became the first modern conductor to be confronted by the question of whether to make cuts in it. Nowadays it is usually given uncut—one sign of the maturity and responsibility that modern performers and audiences bring to Bach. But Mendelssohn did what most conductors for 100 years after him did—he made cuts. He eliminated some of the solo arias and duets; he also orchestrated the recitative passage that begins "And behold, the veil of the temple was rent in twain."

Mendelssohn has been much criticized by later commentators (none at the time complained!) for editing a masterpiece. But his object was to make the work seem alive and vivid to an audience of his own time—an audience that was unaccustomed to sitting through 4 hours of Bach.

Whatever he did, it worked. Felix's sister Fanny Mendelssohn, who sang in the chorus, wrote afterward: "The room had all the air of a church: the deepest quiet and most solemn devotion pervaded the whole; only now and then involuntary utterances of intense emotion were heard."

So overwhelming was the reception that the *Passion* had to be repeated ten days later, which happened to be Bach's 144th birthday. This time extra seats were placed in the lobby and a rehearsal room that opened onto the main hall, so the crowd was even larger than at the first performance. Afterward all the main participants went to Zelter's home for a party, at which toasts were drunk to Mendelssohn, Devrient, Zelter—and Bach.

Mendelssohn continued his proselytizing for Bach's music throughout his life (which ended prematurely at the age of 38). He played his piano music and his organ music; he even improvised a piano "accompaniment" to Bach's Chaconne for Violin Solo for the famous violinist Ferdinand David. This, too, was an act of musicological sacrilege, and yet it brought the great Chaconne to an audience that might otherwise have never known it. Once Mendelssohn invited Gioacchino Rossini, the composer of *The Barber of Seville*, to hear him conduct Bach's *B minor Mass*. "It will be quite fun to see Rossini obliged to admire Sebastian Bach," Mendelssohn observed.

When Mendelssohn moved to Leipzig in 1835 to become the conductor of the Gewandhaus he was disturbed to find that no memorial stone existed on Bach's grave, and he forthwith gave an organ concert to raise funds for it.

Reviewing the recital, which included the great Passacaglia in C minor, Robert Schumann wrote in the journal he edited, the *Neue Zeitschrift für Musik*: "A fine summer evening shone through the church windows; even outside, in the open air, many may have reflected on the wonderful sounds, thinking that there is nothing greater in music than the enjoyment of the double mastery displayed when one master expresses the other. Glory and honor to old and young alike!"

Events like these made thousands of music lovers aware of Bach's music, and performances began cropping up with increasing frequency on the continent and in England. Mendelssohn followed up his Berlin *St. Matthew Passion* with a presentation in Leipzig; and the work was also given in Königsberg, Stettin, and other cities. The house of Schlesinger published the music in a piano reduction, bringing it into people's homes.

Mendelssohn also attempted to pay Bach that most sincere but also insidious compliment—that of imitation. But though he had done so much for Bach, Bach did little for him. Apart from some of his organ music, Mendelssohn's Bachian works are largely sterile. The most ambitious example is his oratorio

St. Paul, with chorales in the style of Bach but lacking his power and conviction. Mendelssohn's musical genius lay in other directions. Considering that he himself was in the forefront of musical romanticism, it is gratifying that he could reach out with such understanding and love to the master of the baroque.

Matthäus or
Matthew?

n what language should the *St. Matthew Passion*
be performed? In Bach's own day, the answer was simple—
German—not because of any musicological considerations,
but because it was the language of the composer, the performers, and the audience alike.

Today the answer given by conductors and performing
groups that present the *St. Matthew* still is German—but
largely on grounds of historical authenticity. Listening to a
performance of this deeply dramatic and devotional work
presented in German—sometimes in bad German—by English-speaking singers to an English-speaking audience, one is
sometimes reminded of Joseph Addison's comment about
Italian opera in London in 1711: "There is no Question but

our great Grand-children will be very curious to know the Reason why their Forefathers used to sit together like an Audience of Foreigners in their own Country ... to hear whole Plays acted before them in a Tongue which they did not understand."

The argument over whether or not opera should be translated is, of course, an ancient one, but the *St. Matthew Passion* has a text far different from the usual operatic libretto, being based upon the appropriate gospel passages describing Jesus' trial and execution, with interpolated arias and choruses written by Bach's friend Picander. For the gospel passages, Bach and Picander went directly to Luther's German translation of the New Testament.

But these musical portions somehow work at least equally well with the masterful King James English translation of the Bible, and to hear this great work presented in a language that is as understandable as it is beautiful can be an enthralling experience. Yet it is an experience unobtainable even on records, for of the dozen recordings currently available, every one of them is in German—the *Matthäuspassion* rather than the *St. Matthew Passion*.

A conductor who believed the *St. Matthew Passion* should be presented in the language of its audience was Bruno Walter, who died in 1962. As conductor of the Leipzig Gewandhaus in the 1930s Walter used to give regular Eastertime performances of the *St. Matthew*, naturally in German, and after he came to the United States as a refugee from the Nazis he decided to resume the practice in New York—but this time in English. "The words, in conjunction with the music, should make an immediate emotional impression upon the listener," he wrote.

So for three years during World War II Bruno Walter

gave uncut English-language performances of Bach's *St. Matthew Passion* with the Philharmonic Symphony Society of New York (as it was then called) and the Westminster Choir in Carnegie Hall. Some of the artists involved were Nadine Conner, soprano; William Hain, tenor; Mack Harrell, baritone; Ralph Kirkpatrick, harpsichordist, and Janos Starker, viola da gambist. The performances lasted 4 hours, with a half-hour break in the middle during which the audience took brief refreshment—some at the Automat then located down the block on 57th Street.

For at least one young person in that audience, Bruno Walter's *St. Matthew Passion* in English was an indelible experience, a memory that has lasted a lifetime. True, Walter is no longer around, and perhaps neither are conductors like him. But the English language is still here, and one longs to hear it once again put to so noble a use.

Mr. Wesley Meets Mr. Bach

etween the death of Henry Purcell in 1695 and the birth of Edward Elgar in 1857 Great Britain produced no major composers—a lack it made up by enthusiastically cultivating a number of foreign geniuses, among them Handel, Haydn, and Mendelssohn. London also played host to Mozart as a child, and the Philharmonic Society invited Beethoven to come there.

Bach and his music, on the other hand, were unknown in England, not only during his lifetime but for several decades thereafter. Handel's long years of residence in London left a lasting influence upon British musical life, so that there hardly seemed room for another Germanic baroque composer.

However, word of the legendary organist who left behind

him a few not unworthy compositions began to seep through. Bach's youngest son, Johann Christian, settled in London and became music master to the Queen; while he himself wrote in the new "galant" style rather than the polyphony of his father, he at least carried the name Bach to a new country. Two German organists, Carl Friedrich Horn (1762–1830) and August Friedrich Christoph Kollmann (1756–1829), moved to London, becoming organists respectively at St. George's Chapel at Windsor and St. James's in London. Both played Bach's music. Joining them was an English organist, Benjamin Jacob (1778–1829), who also had a taste for Bach and included his works on 4-hour-long "organ exhibitions" he instituted. Sometimes audiences of up to 5,000 came to these concerts.

But the main instigator of British interest in Bach's music was Samuel Wesley (1766–1837), nephew of John Wesley, the preacher and minister whose name is commemorated in the branch of Methodism he helped to establish. Samuel Wesley was a composer and organist of such skill that he came to be regarded as the father of modern English organ playing. He also was one of those charming eccentrics which Britain seems to produce with particular frequency. In his young days he suffered an accidental injury to his brain as the result of a fall; although it interfered with his activities from time to time he nevertheless continued performing and proselytizing for Bach to the end of his life. He fathered an illegitimate son, whom he named Samuel Sebastian Wesley; he, too, became a celebrated organist.

Samuel Wesley was a child prodigy and a prolific composer, but he devoted much of his life to working tirelessly on behalf of "Saint Sebastian," as he called Bach, playing his music, lecturing, and corresponding with other musicians. In 1875 his daughter Eliza Wesley published a slim but elegant volume entitled *Samuel Wesley's Famous Bach Letters*, writing in her introduction: "It was to his discernment and zealous perseverance that Bach's transcendent genius was made known and appreciated (although tardily and through much opposition) by the English musical world."

Wesley's main opposition to furthering Bach's music came from Dr. Charles Burney, the famous English musical traveler and author of a still extant *General History of Music*. Burney didn't exactly dislike Bach, but he found his music difficult and ungraceful; he much preferred the works of Bach's sons and of his particular idol, George Frideric Handel.

In his letters, which are addressed to Benjamin Jacob, Wesley, in a vigorous, almost boisterous prose style, denounces "the blind worship of Handel" and "all the prejudiced Handelians" he says are blocking the appreciation of Bach's music. He writes to Jacob that he is "rejoiced to find that you are likely to regard his Works with me as a musical Bible unrivaled and inimitable," and finally cries out: "Old Wig forever!"

Wesley and Jacob together prepared the first English edition of *The Well-Tempered Clavier*, which was published in installments starting in 1810, and he worked with Horn to bring out an English translation of Forkel's biography in 1820. Thanks to his pioneering work Bach's music was taken up by British choral societies and eventually became a staple of concert life. The British have never lost their love for Handel, but "Old Wig" has now gained at least an equal footing with him in their musical lives.

Bach and Schweitzer

f all the places in which Bach's music has been played, few are stranger than Lambaréné, a jungle settlement in Gabon, or, as it used to be known, French Equatorial Africa. The performer was almost as unlikely as the locale— an Alsatian physician and scholar who had left a European career to serve as a medical missionary among the African natives.

Albert Schweitzer was eventually to become famous as the jungle doctor, the theologian who wrote *The Quest for the Historical Jesus*, the philosopher who conceived the doctrine of "reverence for life." But music lovers knew Schweitzer long before the rest of the world caught up to him—both as an organist and as the author of a biography of Bach that,

75 years after its publication, remains a stimulating and thoughtful study.

Schweitzer wrote his biography, which he entitled *J. S. Bach, Le Musicien-Poète*, while he was still in medical school in Strasbourg, before he had decided that his vocation lay in Africa. He first discovered Bach's music in 1890 when he was 15 years old, being introduced to it by his teacher, Eugène Münch (an uncle of the French conductor Charles Munch), with whom he had gone to study in Mulhouse. (Writers attempting to strengthen the connection between Schweitzer and Bach have sometimes identified Mulhouse, whose German name is Mülhausen, with the town of Mühlhausen where Bach was organist in his youth. Actually they are two different places, separated by an extra "h" and a few hundred miles.)

Schweitzer learned to play the organ from Charles Widor, the great French organist, in Paris. Widor, impressed by his pupil's knowledge of Bach, urged him to undertake a study of the man and his music "with the French public in mind." Schweitzer's book, published in 1904 when he was not quite 30 years old, was accordingly written in French. A demand immediately arose for a German edition. Schweitzer tried, but found it difficult to translate his thoughts into German. So he wrote an entirely new book in German, a task that took two years. The German edition totalled 844 pages, the French 455. An English edition, revised and expanded at Schweitzer's request—he himself spoke no English—was subsequently issued, so in effect there are three Schweitzer biographies of Bach.

Schweitzer's concept of Bach as a "musician-poet," expressed in the title of the French edition, added a dimension to the picture of a composer so often regarded as austere and aloof. "Mozart," Schweitzer wrote, "is purely a musician; he takes a given text and clothes it in a beautiful melody. Bach, on the other hand, digs in it; he explores it thoroughly until he has found the idea which in his eyes represents the heart of it and which he will have to illustrate in music."

Schweitzer's activities on behalf of Bach extended beyond writing about him; he also was instrumental in the founding of the Bach Society of Paris in 1905, and gave organ recitals in several European countries. It was at a Bach concert in Barcelona that the King of Spain asked him whether it was difficult to play the organ. "Almost as difficult," Schweitzer replied, "as to rule Spain."

That Schweitzer should choose to spend his life working in Africa was perfectly consistent with his ideals and his character; that he should do so without, in effect, taking Bach with him, was unthinkable. Just before he left in 1913 the Paris Missionary Society presented him with a zinc-lined piano with an organ-pedal attachment, specially designed for the tropics. And amid the sounds of the jungle Schweitzer would play the music of Bach, Mendelssohn, Widor, and others every evening after his day's work in his little hospital of corrugated iron on the banks of the Ogowe River at Lambaréné.

Not all of Schweitzer's music making was confined to Africa; during his periodic returns to Europe he also played the organ in his home church at Gunsbach in Alsace. To admirers who wrote to him asking for a picture he would generally send one of himself inscribed "At the organ in Gunsbach." Schweitzer made a number of organ recordings during his returns to Europe, and in 1949, on his only trip to the United States, to appear at a Goethe Festival in Aspen, Colorado, he played Bach on organs in several American cities.

The only time he declined an opportunity to join a Bach festivity was in 1935 when the city of Leipzig marked the 250th anniversary of the composer's birth. Schweitzer refused to go to Germany during the Nazi era.

Schweitzer died at Lambaréné in 1965 at the age of 90. Not least among his extraordinary accomplishments, perhaps, is that he is the only musician ever to have won the Nobel Peace Prize.

Bach in America

ach's music is in the air; it has flown westward on the wings of the English language." So wrote Hubert J. Foss, chief of the music department of the Oxford University Press, in a report from America to the *Musical Times* of London on November 1, 1930. Foss detailed some of Bach's music he had heard in the United States: the *B minor Mass*, *The Art of the Fugue* in Wolfgang Graeser's orchestration; several transcriptions by Leopold Stokowski with the Philadelphia Orchestra.

Had Foss, or his equivalent, visited the United States a century earlier, his report would have been far less enthusiastic. Bach was a late arrival in America, reaching these shores well after his old rival Handel, not to mention Haydn,

Mozart, Beethoven, and Mendelssohn, all of whom were performed by the musical organizations that then existed.

Even the Moravian communities of Pennsylvania, which performed European music before other areas, were ignorant of J. S. Bach. By 1743 a small orchestra was functioning in Bethlehem, Pennsylvania; on its programs in later years were works by Carl Philipp Emanuel Bach and Johann Christian Bach, but none by Sebastian. A composer named Johann Friedrich Peter arrived in Bethlehem from Holland in 1770 with copies of music by Johann Christoph Friedrich Bach; again nothing by the great Bach. In Boston the Handel and Haydn Society presented Handel's *Messiah* in 1818; it was not until 1874 that they got around to Bach's *St. Matthew Passion*.

The propagation of Bach in America, as in England, was largely the work of one man. John Frederick Wolle, a conductor and organist, was born in Bethlehem in 1863. By that time printed editions of Bach's organ and clavier music had begun to arrive in small amounts from publishers in Germany and England.

The music fascinated Wolle who, at the age of 19, began playing it at churches in Bethlehem and Easton, where he served as organist. Subsequently he spent several years studying in Munich, and upon his return redoubled his activities on behalf of Bach's music, both in Pennsylvania and in California, where he was a professor at the University of California from 1905 to 1911. Wolle put on performances of the *St. John Passion* in 1888 and of the *St. Matthew* in 1892, both in Bethlehem.

Wolle was the organizer of the Bach Choir of Bethlehem which, on March 27, 1900, gave the first complete performance in the United States of the *Mass in B minor*. This was the beginning of the Bethlehem Bach Festival, which continues to this day every May on the campus of Lehigh University, and which has served as a model for many Bach festivals that have sprung up since.

A parallel movement took place toward performances of Bach's instrumental music in American concert halls, again thanks largely to the efforts of a single individual, Theodore Thomas. The German-born Thomas led his own orchestra through inland cities for many years, traveling what became known as the "Thomas Highway"; he also served later as conductor of the New York Philharmonic and the Chicago Symphony. Bach was unknown to American symphonic audiences; even in England it took until 1845 before the London Philharmonic first listed his name on a program, performing the Suite No. 3 in D, with Felix Mendelssohn conducting.

Thomas gave the United States premiere of the Suite in D in 1876—the first time the Air for the G String had ever been heard in America. He was an adherent of the theory that baroque music sounded best with inflated forces. In 1881 he gave the cantata "A Mighty Fortress" with the entire New York Philharmonic and a 500-voice choir; for the *B minor Mass* in 1902 he employed 131 instrumentalists. Thomas spent 15 years with the New York Philharmonic. Over that period he raised Bach to the orchestra's eighth most frequently played composer, with a total of thirteen performances. (Preceding him were Beethoven, Wagner, Schumann, Schubert, Mozart, Anton Rubinstein, and Brahms; following were Liszt, Berlioz, Dvořák, and Weber.)

Leopold Stokowski, who came to the United States from his native England in 1905, took up where Thomas left off. Stokowski's first American post was as organist and choirmaster at St. Bartholomew's Church, then on Madison Avenue and Forty-fourth Street in New York. Stokowski, who had become familiar with Bach's music in England, introduced the congregants of St. Bart's to such works as the Toccata and Fugue in D minor, the "Big" and "Little" Fugues in G minor, and even selections from *The Well-Tempered Clavier*, which he performed on the organ. It is curious that Stokowski began his career by transcribing Bach's music *to* rather than *from* the organ, which was his later practice as a symphonic conductor (see Hyphenated Bach). On April 10 and 17, 1907, Stokowski directed the *St. Matthew Passion* at St. Bartholomew's after drilling his performers for nearly a year in a work totally unfamiliar to them.

When Stokowski became conductor of the Philadelphia Orchestra in 1912 he went right on playing Bach, mainly in transcription form. In time, the Brandenburg concertos and a few other Bach orchestral pieces became staples on symphony programs throughout America. But Bach's real musical home has never been in the symphony hall; it has been, rather, at festivals, all-Bach concerts, baroque programs, and other particular events. More than any of the other great composer's, Bach's music seems to flourish in a distinctive, almost festive atmosphere. It creates a special world of its own.

In 1945 an organization called the Bach Aria Group came into being, devoted to the furtherance of perhaps the most neglected major segment of Bach's work, his cantatas. It was the creation of William H. Scheide of Princeton, New Jersey, the heir to an oil fortune, with an interest in musicology and a love of Bach.

Samuel Baron, the flutist who heads the Bach Aria Group's offshoot, the Bach Aria Festival and Institute, recalls that Scheide first began thinking of this project in the 1930s. "The cantatas weren't really known then," says Baron. "They were the last of his music to come into recognition. After the war, Scheide decided the time was ripe. He took ten students up to a camp in Vermont and we worked on the music. We photostated the score from the Bach Gesellschaft collection and then cut the copies into strips for each of the parts. Strips of paper were always flying around, but it was wonderfully exciting."

Starting in 1950 the Bach Aria Group performed annually at Town Hall in New York. It also toured extensively in the United States and traveled to South America, Europe, and Israel. It attracted such well-known singers as soprano Eileen Farrell and tenor Jan Peerce, neither of whom had sung this music before, and it found audiences on the concert-hall and college circuit extremely responsive to music that was, for the most part, entirely unknown to them.

Scheide retired in 1980, but Sam Baron, who had succeeded Julius Baker as the group's first flute in 1965, decided to continue. The Bach Aria Group was reorganized on the campus of the State University of New York at Stony Brook, Long Island, and there every summer a two-week-long festival is held with the participation of leading vocal and instrumental soloists. At the concurrently held Bach Aria Institute young musicians from all over the country attend master classes and seminars on Bach's music. For the ultimate touch, the festival operates a refreshment center called Zimmermann's at Stony Brook.

Bach festivals now abound across the country—Basically Bach at Lincoln Center with Richard Westenburg and Musica Sacra; the Bach Festival at Rollins College in Winter Park, Florida, established in 1935; the New England Bach Festival at Brattleboro, Vermont, directed by Blanche Moyse; the Oregon Bach Festival at the University of Oregon at Eugene, and several dozen others. Considering that he lived and died before the United States of America even existed, an amazing portion of Bach's heritage has found its way to this country.

The Bach Virtuosi

 ore than conductors, it was organists and pianists who kept Bach's music alive during the fallow nineteenth century. To associate Bach with romantic keyboard virtuosi may seem far-fetched, yet many of the emerging breed of piano masters found delight and satisfaction in his music. John Field, born in Dublin in 1782, became one of the most admired pianists in Europe; he played Bach fugues so well that he received ovations from Parisian audiences who were hearing the music for the first time. Frederic Chopin, the epitome of romantic pianists, was another Bach lover; the story went that he warmed up before every concert with a few preludes and fugues from *The Well-Tempered Clavier*. Many of the great virtuosi of the century, including Franz Liszt, knew Bach's music, but most of them preferred to play it in their own transcriptions rather than from the original score.

Among the first to play Bach with a minimum of romantic infusions was the British pianist Harold Samuel. As a result, Samuel became known as a Bach specialist. In 1921 he gave a series of six all-Bach piano recitals in London, then repeated the sequence in New York. No one had done this before, and listeners became aware there was more than one way of playing Bach.

A few years later they also became aware that there was more than one instrument upon which to play him. Wanda Landowska, a Polish-born pianist who had settled in Paris, single-handedly (or rather, double-handedly) revived the harpsichord as a performing instrument in the early 1900s. Since no satisfactory instruments existed, she had them built to her specifications by Pleyel. To Landowska, Bach's keyboard music belonged on the harpsichord, and she proselytized for both the instrument and the composer. Authenticity of sound was undoubtedly part of her performances' appeal, but there was no trace of academia about her rich, lively, and rhythmically propulsive style.

Landowska came to the United States in 1941 after the Nazis had occupied Paris; she had played in America before, but this time she really caught the public fancy as a kind of high priestess of the harpsichord. A small woman in a flowing velvet gown, she gave the impression of communing with her instrument rather than playing it. Through concerts devoted to *The Well-Tempered Clavier* and the *Goldberg Variations*, as well as other pieces, she demonstrated that Bach, played with skill and with love, could be a musical box-office draw.

Landowska's success was so enormous that after her death in 1959 many pianists were almost afraid to play Bach; the

A harpsichord player in the early eighteenth century.

use of a harpsichord for his music became almost obligatory. However, a reaction eventually set in, with Rosalyn Tureck and the late Canadian pianist Glenn Gould among those demonstrating that an enlivening sense of musicianship could achieve its effect on the piano no less than the harpsichord.

Gould was one of the most remarkable pianists of his generation, bringing to his Bach performances a particular flair and enthusiasm along with a consummate musicianship. A great deal of interest centered upon his well-publicized eccentricities. He would soak his hands in hot water for twenty minutes before every recital; he sat in a special adjustable chair slung so low that his knees almost got in the way of his hands at the keyboard; he sighed and sang audibly during his performances; he sipped from a bottle of spring water always at his side. Frail in build, he wrapped himself in coats and scarves and gloves even in summer, and he regularly traveled with a small pharmacopoeia of pills to ward off headache, relieve tension, and maintain circulation.

Whether in spite of or because of these unorthodox customs his Bach performances had a bounce and crystalline clarity like no others; few artists so brilliantly combined technical aplomb and musicianly insight. He somehow blended the "feel" of a harpsichord with the sound of a piano. Young people in particular flocked to his concerts and made him almost a cult figure. Gould himself once said: "There is a bridge between Bach's ideas of rhythm and those of the mid-twentieth century, and it has been created by popular music and jazz."

Gould, who made his U.S. debut in 1955 at the age of 22, startled the musical world in 1964 by withdrawing from concertizing and devoting himself to recording. Music, he said, was best performed and heard in solitude. His own achievements he attributed to his self-imposed isolation from musical fashions and the commerce of concert life or, as he expressed it picturesquely, the "tremendously tyrannical forces of the Zeitgeist."

Gould said he considered recording a distinctive art form. He would record the same music on tape several times, then, acting as his own editor, would select and splice together the parts that added up to the final version he wanted—all without losing the quality of spontaneity that was one of his hallmarks. Many of the recordings he made for Columbia were of Bach—*The Art of the Fugue* on the organ; the *Goldberg Variations*, the French and English Suites, *The Well-Tempered Clavier*, the Toccatas, Inventions and others on the piano.

On October 4, 1982, Glenn Gould, the seeming hypochondriac, died at the age of 50 in a Toronto hospital, following a stroke. He left behind him perhaps the most extensive and significant legacy of recorded Bach ever compiled by a pianist.

Virtuosi on other instruments also achieved reputations as Bach specialists. E. Power Biggs played Bach organ music with a clarity of style and sound free of nineteenth-century Romanticism. Both as cellist and conductor, Pablo Casals brought a special vibrancy to Bach performances throughout his long lifetime. He said that he started every day at the piano, playing Bach preludes and fugues because the music "refreshes the spirit and induces a calm and cheerful frame of mind for the day's activities." On a similar plane, though necessarily more limited, have been Andrés Segovia's arrangements for guitar of many of Bach's pieces written originally for lute, clavier, or violin. With musicians of this quality, just as in Bach's day, choice of instrument seems almost secondary.

Hyphenated Bach

 here's an old story of Ferruccio Busoni, the great pianist, introducing his wife to a stranger at a party who replies politely, "How do you do, Mrs. Bach-Busoni." No doubt the story is apocryphal, but it illustrates the frequency with which the name Bach-Busoni appeared on concert programs during the early years of the twentieth century. Busoni, an overpowering pianist and a respected composer in his own right, was among the many who have transcribed or expanded Bach's music, usually for their own performing purposes. Here are some of the more familiar transcription labels, in chronological order.

Bach–Liszt. Franz Liszt (1811-1871),
    the most spectacular pianist of the nineteenth century,

played Bach (at least in public) only in transcription form. Among his most notable Bach piano transcriptions were six preludes and fugues for organ of which the first, in A minor, was for many years a concert favorite. Actually, he transcribed Bach rather less frequently than he did other composers. He also composed variations of his own on several Bach themes and a Prelude and Fugue on B-A-C-H.

Bach-Gounod. Charles Gounod (1818–1893)
is guilty of only one Bach adaptation. He superimposed a melody of his own over the first prelude, in C major, of *The Well-Tempered Clavier*, turning that flowingly beautiful piece into a mere accompaniment. Gounod first called it *"Méditation sur le premier prélude de Bach"* and said it was only a little joke, but concert audiences went wild for it and it has been known ever since as "Ave Maria."

Bach-Tausig. Carl Tausig (1841–1871)
was Liszt's favorite pupil and carved out a spectacular career for himself in his brief lifetime. His piano arrangement of Bach's organ Toccata and Fugue in D minor once was a concert favorite.

Bach-Busoni. Ferruccio Busoni (1866–1924)
was perfectly capable of playing Bach's keyboard works without transcription, and sometimes did. But he was an inveterate arranger and may have more hyphenated Bach to his credit than any other pianist. He even transcribed the Chromatic Fantasia and Fugue for cello and piano. Seven volumes of "Bach-Busoni" works have been published.

HYPHENATED BACH

Bach-Stokowski.

No Bach arrangements have generated more controversy than those by Leopold Stokowski (1882–1977). As conductor of the Philadelphia Orchestra from 1912 to 1936, he introduced orchestral transcriptions of many of Bach's organ works, such as the Toccata and Fugue in D minor, the Passacaglia and Fugue in C minor, a dozen chorale preludes, and many others. At that time such works could be heard only in organ recitals, which were frequented by few concertgoers, and Stokowski felt with justice that he was introducing them to a wider audience. His arrangements, which some alleged were at least partially the work of the orchestra's bass clarinetist, Lucien Cailliet, abounded in resplendent colors and striking dynamics. "Bach was just a sleepy old man, but a wonderful musician, of course," Stokowski said. "The music appeals to me for what can be done with it."

Critics at the time denounced Stokowski's transcriptions almost as a sacrilege, but a later view is that they not only broadened Bach's appeal but did so in a majestic, moving, and stimulating manner. Stokowski played on the great instrument of his time, the symphony orchestra, with as much skill as Bach had played on his great instrument, the organ.

Updating Bach

hus Bach is the end. Nothing comes from him; everything leads to him." These words by Albert Schweitzer must surely count among the least perceptive of that great musician-humanitarian's observations in his Bach biography. Schweitzer was only half right: Bach did indeed represent the culmination of all music before him, but he has also become a starting point for musicians—particularly twentieth-century musicians—taking off on new departures of their own.

The range of such musical departures has been enormous. Arnold Schoenberg asserted that twelve-tone music, the school of composition that had such a powerful influence in the first half of the century, took its inspiration from Bach. Heitor

Villa-Lobos, the prolific Brazilian composer, created a species of popular works he entitled *Bachianas Brasileras*, of which he wrote: "This is a special kind of musical composition, based on an intimate knowledge of the great works of J. S. Bach and also on the composer's affinity with the harmonic, contrapuntal and melodic atmosphere of the folklore of the northeastern region of Brazil. The composer considers Bach a universal and rich folkloristic source, deeply rooted in the folk music of every country in the world. . . . a mediator among all races."

Bach's influence has also extended to the more popular musical forms, including jazz, rock, and synthesizer creations. Much of Bach's instrumental music combines a strong rhythmic bass foundation with terse contrapuntal melodies—elements that have their parallels in modern forms. In the 1960s, particularly, popular musicians came up with a number of Bach-related works. George Harrison of the Beatles said that a trumpet obbligato in "Penny Lane" had been inspired by the dazzling high-pitched trumpet of the Brandenburg Concerto No. 2. A hit recording of 1967, "A Whiter Shade of Pale," by a group called Procol Harum, was based on the *Wachet auf* cantata. Several groups worked on the concept of "Baroque Rock," which enjoyed at least a temporary vogue.

The Swingle Singers, a French group of eight voices headed by an American, Ward Swingle, popularized a number of Bach pieces by singing them in wordless syllables ("do-do-do-be-do") over the accompaniment of a jazz rhythm section in 4/4 time. Among the works thus treated were preludes, fugues, canons, and inventions. Assembled on a recording called *Bach's Greatest Hits*, the collection became a best-seller.

The most extraordinary of all recordings devoted to updated Bach has been *Switched-On Bach*, a sequence of electronic transcriptions performed on the Moog synthesizer, a device perfected by Robert Moog. *Switched-On Bach*, released by Columbia in 1968, became the first "classical" record in 10 years to win a "Gold Record" Award, signifying sales in excess of $1,000,000.

Switched-On Bach was the creation of a 28-year-old physicist-musician named Walter Carlos, working at the time as a low-paid tape editor with ambitions of establishing himself as a serious composer. Carlos's Bach recordings were the result of hours of painstaking planning, experimenting, taping, and mixing sounds. "We chose Bach," Carlos said at the time, "because he's basically linear and contrapuntal. The synthesizer is a monophonic instrument and has difficulty generating vertical chords. Bach wouldn't care. His attitude was, if you haven't got a violin, play the music on a flute."

Switched-On Bach included the Brandenburg Concerto No. 3, the Air for the G String, *Jesu, Joy of Man's Desiring*, the Choral Prelude *Wachet auf*, and other works. Most of the music was straightforward yet imaginative transcriptions, but sometimes Carlos added personal touches, as in the second movement of the Brandenburg, where two simple chords Bach wrote were elaborated into a sequence of electronic whooshes, swishes, and twittering—a modern version of eighteenth-century improvisation.

In 1972 came the most surprising switch of all. Walter Carlos underwent a sex-change operation, emerging as Wendy Carlos. *Switched-On Bach* continues unaltered, its latest recorded successor being nothing less than the complete Brandenburg concertos.

Curiously, while the trend toward "modernization" of Bach has progressed, a parallel retrograde movement toward "antiquization" has also developed. Organizations like the Academy of Ancient Music of London, Concentus Musicus of Vienna, and Aston Magna of Great Barrington, Massachusetts, among others, have presented successful performances of Bach, employing instruments that approximate those of his own time and observing eighteenth-century stylistic practices. Listeners today may enjoy a variety of Bach performances far wider than that available to any previous generation, including Bach's own.

The Lost Bach

ith more than a thousand works in the Bach catalogue there might hardly seem room for additional entries. Yet a great many works by Bach are believed to have been lost, for though there are allusions to them in documents by his contemporaries they have never turned up. After his death his manuscripts were taken either by his wife or his sons. Anna Magdalena was forced to sell some to gain sustenance, but most of these went to the St. Thomas's School, where they were preserved. Carl Philipp Emanuel carefully retained his portion, which has survived. Bach's oldest son, Wilhelm Friedemann, was less conscientious and, especially in his last years, when he began to drink heavily, sold many of his manuscripts, often for slight sums of money, and a large number of these have disappeared.

THE LOST BACH

Following is a breakdown of Bach compositions that have been lost:

A *Passion According to St. Mark* (only fragments survive).

A *Passion According to St. Luke* (a score of this name exists, but is regarded as spurious; however, Bach apparently did compose a *St. Luke Passion* that has been lost).

Approximately 100 cantatas, both sacred and secular.

"A considerable quantity" of orchestral music, according to the *New Grove Dictionary of Music and Musicians*.

Possibilities of any of this music being recovered had long been regarded as slight. Since it all was in manuscript form, and probably copied out by others at that, positive identification through handwriting might seem almost impossible. Still, discoveries continue to be made. On December 18, 1984, Christoph Wolff, a Harvard musicologist, announced he had unearthed a trove of thirty-three organ preludes by Bach in a collection of eighteenth-century manuscripts at Yale University. Are similar finds likely in the future? Certainly scholars will never give up the quest.

P. D. Q.: The Prodigal Son

eter Schickele is burly, bearded, and blue-eyed, and a familiar figure on the American concert stage. He is a prolific and successful composer who has written everything from soundtracks to operas. However—somewhat to his chagrin—it is not as a serious composer that he is best-known, but in his role as P. D. Q. Bach, "last but least" of the sons of the great Johann. Schickele has never spelled out the given names* of this fictive composer, but P. D. Q. Bach over the last 20 years has developed into one of the most successful spoofs, both commercially and artistically, that music has ever known.

*Webster's Ninth New Collegiate Dictionary lists PDQ as an abbreviation for "pretty damn quick."

P. D. Q.: THE PRODIGAL SON

"Most satirists make fun of what they like, not what they don't like," says Schickele, who was born in Ames, Iowa, in 1935, and studied music at Swarthmore College and the Juilliard School. "I wound up doing a satire on Bach and Mozart because they are the two composers I love the most. P. D. Q., as you might say, falls between them."

Schickele began putting on his musical satires in 1959, when he was still at Juilliard, starting with a work he called the Concerto for Horn and Hardart. "The pieces I did then were just for fun; I never attached a particular identity to them," he says. "But after a year or two, I realized that P. D. Q. Bach must have written them. The first public concert with his name on the program was at Town Hall in New York on April 24, 1965."*

This and subsequent concerts featured works such as the cantata *Iphigenia in Brooklyn*, the oratorio *The Seasonings*, Pervertimento, Schleptet, the Fuga Vulgaris from the *Toot Suite*, and the half-act opera *The Stoned Guest*. All these works, Schickele reported solemnly, were discovered among P. D. Q.'s "police records and tavern IOUs."

Schickele carried his satire on musicological research a step further in his jacket notes for the first LP recording of P. D. Q. Bach's music, on the Vanguard label: "In 1953, while visiting the lovely Lechendochschloss in Bavaria, Prof. Schickele discovered—quite by chance, in all fairness—a piece of manuscript being used as a strainer in the caretaker's percolator. This turned out to be the 'Sanka' Cantata, the first autograph manuscript by P. D. Q. Bach ever found. . . . Almost overnight, what had been neglect turned into overwhelming avoidance on the part of music lovers every-

*It may (or may not) be significant that the twentieth anniversary of P. D. Q. Bach's debut followed by one month the 300th birthday of J. S. Bach.

161

where. . . ." In 1976 Schickele published *The Definitive Biography of P. D. Q. Bach (1807-1742)?*, undoubtedly the last word on the subject.

Schickele, who lives with his wife and two children in Brooklyn (where else would P. D. Q. Bach live nowadays?), divides the year between his own music and his protégé's. He makes about fifty appearances annually as P. D. Q. Bach in concert halls and on college campuses, and says he is a little surprised at his continuing success.

"I thought P. D. Q.'s career might last five years at most, but it has gone on for twenty," he says. "I recently counted up how many works there are and was amazed to find that there are over seventy pieces in the P. D. Q. catalogue. That's really composing! I don't think I'm scraping the bottom of the barrel yet; I'm still having fun and I hope to go on doing so. P. D. Q. Bach is far from washed up."

Fair warning.

Bach's Puntheon

One of the more pleasant, if unimportant, aspects of Bach is the ease with which his name lends itself to punning in two languages, German and English. The German word "Bach" means "brook" in English, so the English equivalent of Bach's full name would be John Sebastian Brook.

The most famous of Bach puns is Ludwig van Beethoven's tribute: "Not *Bach* (brook) but *Meer* (ocean) should be his name." Bach himself is alleged to be the author of at least one pun. Speaking of a favorite pupil named Johann Ludwig Krebs, he said: "He is the only crab (*Krebs*) in this brook (*Bach*)."

Most modern English puns have been somewhat less elegant:

During the 1930s Leopold Stokowski's orchestral transcriptions of Bach's organ music were labeled "Bachowski."

The Bach Festival of the Bach Aria Group at Stony Brook, Long Island, winds up its activities every summer with a party called a Bacchanalia.

The New England Bach Festival, held every autumn at foliage time in Brattleboro, Vermont, has as one of its themes Bach to Nature.

The Oregon Bach Festival every summer in Eugene puts up a Bach's Lunch for its patrons.

CBS Records issues a series of releases entitled Bach's Tops.

The Chamber Music Society of Lincoln Center entitled its 1984 televised comparison of Bach played on ancient and modern instruments Bach to Bach.

The Eliot Feld Ballet has introduced a new dance work called Play Bach.

And so it goes, Bach and forth.

The Making of a Bach Specialist

he emergence of musicians who make flourishing careers as Bach specialists is a comparatively recent phenomenon. Rosalyn Tureck, one of the most successful of the breed, recalls that when she first proposed giving a series of all-Bach recitals at Town Hall in New York in 1937, managers tried to discourage her.

"They said I'd lose my shirt, that Bach was impossible at the box office, that it wouldn't go," she says. "Well, it did go. I gave one concert a week for six weeks, playing all of the Forty-eight, the *Goldberg Variations*, the Partitas, the Suites. I couldn't afford six evenings in Town Hall, so most of the concerts were on Wednesday afternoons. People came, and we finished in the black."

Tureck, who was 22 at the time, for some years pursued parallel careers as a Bach specialist and as an all-around pianist. Born in Chicago, she studied there and at Juilliard in New York, where she later also taught. In her early years she played the Brahms B-flat Concerto with the Philadelphia Orchestra and the Beethoven *Emperor* with the New York Philharmonic.

"There was a good deal of ignorance about Bach in those days," she says. "When I would talk about the *Goldberg Variations* at Juilliard, students would ask: 'Who is this composer Goldberg?'

"I started playing Bach early. He was one of the composers given to me by my first teacher, Sophia Brilliant-Liven, a Russian immigrant who had been a teaching assistant to Anton Rubinstein. I was mooning over Bach's music by the age of 10. I didn't know it was supposed to be more difficult than Mendelssohn. My second teacher, Jan Chiapusso, the Bach scholar, told me: 'My God, girl, if you can do this, you ought to specialize in Bach.' So I started studying the organ, the harpsichord and the clavichord. I learned the Forty-eight at the rate of three a week. When the auditions committee at Juilliard asked me to play one of the *Well-Tempered Clavier* preludes and fugues, I said, 'Which one would you like to hear?' "

After graduating from Juilliard Tureck entered the Naumburg Competition in New York and reached the finals. At her decisive audition she played an all-Bach program—and lost. "The jurors felt they couldn't give me the award because they were sure that nobody could make a career in Bach," she says.

While Tureck achieved a measure of recognition in the United States as a young pianist, it was in Europe that she really established herself as a Bach performer, especially with a sequence of three all-Bach recitals in London in 1953. British audiences were unaccustomed to hearing Bach played on the piano with such crisp, clear articulation. In a typical review, Clive Barnes, then a critic for the *London Daily Express*, wrote: "Her playing is as logical as architecture and as mysterious as poetry." She moved to London, toured extensively through Europe, and made occasional appearances in the United States. While in England she published a three-volume *Introduction to the Performance of Bach* and also founded an International Bach Society. In the mid-1970s she returned to the United States, making New York the headquarters for her performing and research activities.

In 1977 Tureck recreated at Carnegie Hall her Town Hall Bach marathon of 40 years before. In the 1984–1985 season she observed the Bach Tercentenary with another series of six Carnegie Hall concerts, culminating in a double performance of the *Goldberg Variations* on both harpsichord and piano, with a dinner break between.

Tureck says she has never regretted her concentration on Bach. "He engages every single faculty," she explains. "He's never easy. But he's never boring. No other composer compares with him in holding your interest concert after concert. I believe Bach is part of the texture of our world just as James Joyce is. Joyce's writing is contrapuntal; it destroys vertical thinking just as Bach's music does. With Bach you don't really live in the past."

Although it is as a Bach pianist that she has established her position, Tureck says she has no strong feelings about what instrument his music should be played on. "Bach was an abstract composer and instruments are secondary," she says. "He wrote his music as music, independent of specific sonorities. That's why it can 'sound' on so many instruments. There's a universal error that it is the rhythmic element in Bach's music that makes it so adaptable, but that's not so. It's not one-step music; it is very subtle rhythmically, full of variety.

"How can you say there is a 'right' instrument for Bach, when he wrote the same work for organ, harpsichord and violin, when he transferred so much music from one medium to the other? To be sure, this was a thrifty thing to do, but Bach was no musical miser; his reusing of material had its own musical validity. That was true even when he was using music by other composers. Being the genius that he was, everything got better when he turned his hand to it.

"I've played Bach's music on the clavichord, the harpsichord, the piano and the Moog. It doesn't matter which instrument you play—it's all a matter of style. No matter *what* instrument they invent, Bach will be ready to be played on it."

Rosalyn Tureck was asked what she thought Bach might have done had he been born 300 years later. Would he have composed Hollywood soundtracks, or perhaps television jingles?

"No, I don't think so," she replied. "Bach would always have been a contemporary composer, but not a popular composer. He always attached himself to an institution—a court, a church, or a school. So I think that today he probably would have been connected with a university, and gone on writing serious music. There would be one big difference—today he would be collecting royalties."

Bach in Literature

iterary allusions to Bach, like the general appreciation of his music, began to appear in the late nineteenth century and have become more numerous in the twentieth. Here are some examples, arranged alphabetically by author.

Are all men born to play Bach's fiddle-fugues?

—Robert Browning: *Mr. Sludge, "The Medium."* The words are used in the sense of "Can all men perform difficult feats?" In the poem Mr. Sludge, a professional medium, defends his trade as a charlatan.

"And are you still as fond of music as ever, Mr. Pontifex?" said Miss Skinner to Ernest during the course of lunch.

"Of some kinds of music, yes, Miss Skinner, but you know I never did like modern music. . . . I would like modern music, if I could; I have been trying all my life to like it, but I succeed less and less the older I grow."

"And pray, where do you consider modern music to begin?"

"With Sebastian Bach."

> —Samuel Butler: *The Way of All Flesh*.
> Samuel Butler was a devoted
> Handelian, and Mr. Pontifex reflects
> his creator's view.

The musical-hall singer attends a series
Of masses and fugues and "ops"
  By Bach, interwoven
  With Spohr and Beethoven,
At classical Monday Pops.

> —W.S. Gilbert: *The Mikado*. Judging by his
> inclusion in the Mikado's list of
> punishments that fit the crime, Bach was
> coming into vogue in the London of
> 1885. Ludwig Spohr, on the other hand,
> was going out of vogue and his music is
> little heard today.

The fact that the Matthew Passion, for example, the Hammerklavier Sonata, had had human authors was a source of hope. It was just conceivable that humanity might some day and somehow be made a little more John-Sebastian-like. If there were no Well-Tempered Clavichord, why should one bother even to wish for revolutionary changes?

—Aldous Huxley: *Eyeless in Gaza*

She played Bach. I do not know the names of the pieces, but I recognized the stiff ceremonial of the frenchified little German courts and the sober, thrifty comfort of the burghers, and the dancing on the village green, the green trees that looked like Christmas trees, and the sunlight on the wide German country, and a tender cosiness; and in my nostrils there was a warm scent of the soil and I was conscious of a sturdy strength that seemed to have its roots deep in mother earth, and of an elemental power that was timeless and had no home in space.

—W. Somerset Maugham: *The Alien Corn*

The committee—now a permanent body—
   formed to do but one thing,
discover positions for artists, was worried, then happy;
rejoiced to have magnetized Bach and his family
   "to Northwestern," besides five harpsichords
      without which he would not leave home. . . .
Haydn, when he had heard of Bach's billowing sail,
begged Prince Esterházy to lend him to Yale.

—Marianne Moore: *Dream* (excerpt). The
      poem is a commentary on academic
      appointments for artists.

Thus KANG HI
Who played the spinet on Johnnie Bach's birthday
do not exaggerate/ he at least played on some such
instrument. . . .

> —Ezra Pound: *Canto LIX.*

"Here! none of that mathematical music!'
Said the Kommandant when Münch offered Bach to
the regiment.

> —Ezra Pound: *Canto LXXX.* Pound's
> Cantos have a number of references to
> Bach. These are two of the more
> intelligible.

There are times when, to paint a complete portrait
of someone, we should have to add a phonetic imitation to our verbal description, and our portrait of
M. de Charlus presented is liable to remain incomplete
in the absence of that little laugh, so delicate, so light,
just as certain works of Bach are never accurately
rendered because our orchestras lack those small high
trumpets, with a sound so entirely their own, for
which their composer wrote this or that part.

> —Marcel Proust: *Cities of the Plain.* Proust's
> writings abound in musical allusions,
> Bach among them. This and the two
> following extracts are from the
> multivolume *Remembrance of Things Past.*

Such was, along with great civility and, when they
were talking, a deaf insistence on not letting them-

selves be interrupted, on picking up twenty times right where they had been if one did interrupt, thus giving their conversation the unshakeable solidity of a Bach fugue, the character of the inhabitants of this tiny village. . . .

—Marcel Proust: *Cities of the Plain*.

Then at once M. de Norpois began to speak about one thing and another, no longer afraid to make a noise as, when the last note of a sublime aria by Bach has died away, the audience are no longer afraid to talk aloud, to call for their hats and coats in the cloakroom.

—Marcel Proust: *The Fugitive*.

He could hear the thunders of Johann Sebastian Bach's oceanic soul: the winds and storms, the gusts and scudding clouds, the peoples intoxicated with joy, fury, or pain . . . he could hear the roaring fountainhead of thoughts, passions, and musical forms; of heroic life, Shakespearean hallucinations, and Savonarola-like prophecies; of visions—pastoral, epic, or apocalyptic—that were contained within the narrow frame of the small-statured cantor from Thuringia, with his bright eyes and double chin, his upturning brows and wrinkled lids. He could readily see him— somber, jovial, a trifle ridiculous; at once Gothic and rococo, quick to anger, stubborn, serene, gripped by a passion for life and a nostalgia for death.

—Romain Rolland: *Jean-Christophe in Paris*.

Basically Bach

My music-loving Self this afternoon
(Clothed in the gilded surname of Sassoon)
Squats in the packed Sheldonian and observes
An intellectual bee-hive perched and seated
In achromatic and expectant curves
Of buzzing, sunbeam-flecked, and overheated
Accommodation. Skins perspire . . . but hark! . . .
Begins the great *B minor Mass* of Bach.

The choir sings *Gloria in excelsis Deo*
With confident and well-conducted *brio.*
Outside, a motor-bike makes impious clatter,
Impinging on our Eighteenth-Century trammels.
. . . .

Hosanna in excelsis chants the choir
In pious contrapuntal jubilee.
Hosanna shrill the birds in sunset fire
And Benedictus sings my heart to Me.

         —Siegfried Sassoon: *Sheldonian*
            Soliloquy. During Bach's B minor Mass
            (excerpt).

Toward the 400th

 hat his music would be universally played, studied, and written about 300 years after his birth is an idea that probably never crossed the mind of Johann Sebastian Bach. When he thought of immortality, he did so in terms of his soul rather than his music.

Yet this is not to say that Bach had no inkling of the quality of that music, or of the possibility that it would be performed, at least for a time, after his death. He was well aware that music often outlived its creators, if only because he himself had studied, played, and in so many cases adapted the music of the past. He surely knew enough to know that he was a great composer—though how great may have been beyond his comprehension. Even he, with all his intuition and shrewdness, could hardly have conceived that those works written for the courts of Weimar and Cöthen or the churches and coffee houses of Leipzig, or even for the delectation and instruction of his own family at home, would ever be performed for audiences of thousands at great halls in distant lands.

One reason why Bach's music speaks to us today is that it reaches beyond its eighteenth-century origins and trappings. Music in Bach's day was an adjunct, designed for courtly diversion or religious worship. For most people today, music exists by and for itself, unencumbered by court or by church, a matter of individual enjoyment.

This idea of music existing alone—not in a vacuum but in the human mind—was also Bach's. Even his "practical" works, like the Preludes and Fugues of *The Well-Tempered Clavier*, written to demonstrate equal temperament, or the *Goldberg Variations*, intended to assuage insomnia, seem to inhabit a sphere of their own, with their original purpose forgotten. And in his final masterpieces, the *Musical Offering* and *The Art of the Fugue*, Bach really cuts himself loose from all worldly moorings and writes music that exists only as music.

In this respect, as well as in others, Bach is the most "modern" of the great composers. His music can be heard virtually everywhere, in the symphony hall when an orchestra undertakes the Brandenburg concertos or the suites for orchestra; in a solo keyboard or chamber recital, when any of a hundred pieces may be played; in a church that performs the cantatas; at great choral concerts where one of the Passions or oratorios is given; at one of the numerous Bach Festivals—there seem to be more of them every year, both in Europe and America—where scholars, students, and ordinary concertgoers join in an adventure of exploration and discovery.

Most satisfying of all—and this might have surprised and pleased him most of all—Bach can be enjoyed in the home. Thanks to the art of recording, Bach's music has entered the lives of listeners of recent decades to an extent possible at no time before in history, including Bach's own. Hardly a scrap of his music has been left unrecorded, so that the list of his LPs occupies twelve pages in the *Schwann Record & Tape Guide*—more than any other composer. There currently are eight available versions of *The Art of the Fugue* (performed by everything from solo harpsichord to full orchestra), twelve of the *Musical Offering*, sixteen of the Chromatic Fantasia and Fugue, and forty of the complete Brandenburg concertos. The church cantatas, the last relatively unexplored Bach frontier, now are being recorded systematically. Even poor Anna Magdalena has lost exclusive proprietorship of the little musical notebook her husband lovingly compiled for her—there now are half a dozen recordings of it.

Many of Bach's compositions, with their blend of intimacy and complexity, are even better suited to listening in the quiet of the home than in the bustle of the concert hall. Like all great music, they grow richer and more rewarding with repeated hearing.

That, indeed, has been the story of Bach's music over the centuries. The more each generation has heard his music, the more it has loved it and played it. Thanks to recordings, thanks to the spread of music generally, thanks to the upsurge of festivals and the labors of scholars, this generation may be closer to a true understanding of Bach than any that has gone before.

No one can foretell what instruments Bach will be performed on, or how his music will be preserved, or in what locales it will be heard by the time his 400th anniversary rolls around. But if there is any music left in that distant world—or indeed anything left at all—one may be certain that Bach will occupy, as he does now, its vital center.

Appendixes

A BACH CHRONOLOGY

1685   Born in Eisenach, Thuringia, March 21.

1694   Death of his mother.

1695   Death of his father. Goes to live in Ohrdruf with his brother Johann Christoph.

1700   Moves to Lüneburg to attend school there.

1702   Visits Hamburg to hear Reinken play the organ and Celle to hear the French-style court orchestra.

1703   Goes to Weimar for a short-lived job as violinist; then to Arnstadt to become a church organist.

1705   Travels to Lübeck to hear Buxtehude play the organ and also to size up his marriageable daughter.

1707   Takes job in Mühlhausen as organist at St. Blasius's. Marries Maria Barbara Bach, aged 23.

1708   Settles in Weimar as chamber musician at the ducal court; begins raising a family.

1717   Competition with Marchand ends in victory by default. Is imprisoned by the duke of Weimar for accepting another job.

1717   Begins nearly 6 productive years in service of Prince Leopold of Anhalt-Cöthen, with output including the Brandenburg concertos and other instrumental music for clavier, violin, and flute.

1720   Returns from a trip to Carlsbad to find that his wife has died unexpectedly during his absence.

1721   Remarried to Anna Magdalena Wülcken, a professional singer, aged 20.

1722   Writes the first *Little Clavier Book* for his new wife; completes part I of *The Well-Tempered Clavier*.

1723   Becomes cantor at Leipzig, a post he holds to the end of his life. Produces a tremendous outpouring of church cantatas over the next 5 years.

1729   First performance of the *St. Matthew Passion* gets mixed reviews from Leipzig churchgoers.

1730   Irritated by problems with schoolboys and quarrels with Town Council, he writes to his friend Georg Erdmann about possibility of a job elsewhere; none is forthcoming.

1731   Meets Johann Adolf Hasse and his singer-wife Faustina Bordoni at the opera in Dresden; they become friends.

1736   Appointed court composer by the elector of Saxony and king of Poland, Friedrich Augustus II; to prove his worth as a musician, he sends him the *Mass in B minor*.

1740   Failing eyesight troubles him increasingly.

1744   Completes part II of *Well-Tempered Clavier*.

1747   Visits Frederick the Great at Potsdam; composes the *Musical Offering*.

1748   Begins work on *The Art of the Fugue*, his last masterpiece.

1750   Unsuccessful eye operations by the "Chevalier" Taylor. Dies at home July 28, aged 65.

A BACH GLOSSARY

Art of the Fugue   Sometimes, the *Art of Fugue*. A prodigious work of Bach's last years, consisting of canons and fugues on the same theme. Left unfinished.

Bach Gesellschaft   Or, Bach Society. Founded in 1850 to publish Bach's music, which it did over 50 years in forty-six volumes. In 1900 the Neue (New) Bach Gesellschaft was established to publish performing editions and otherwise assist in the encouragement of Bach's music. The American chapter is called the New Bach Society.

Baroque   Roughly, the period between 1600 and 1750. Its music masters include Bach, Handel, Telemann, Vivaldi, Rameau, Couperin, and Purcell, among others.

Brandenburg concertos   Six concertos for varying orchestral combinations dedicated by Bach to the margrave of Brandenburg in 1721.

BWV   Initials for *Bach-Werke-Verzeichnis*, "Bach Work Number." A system of cataloguing and designating Bach's compositions devised by Wolfgang Schmieder in 1950.

Canon   A composition in which the same melody is repeated by voices or instruments each entering before the previous voice has finished.

Cantata   A choral composition of several movements, often with solo vocal parts and usually with orchestral accompaniment. Bach composed over 300.

Chaconne   Originally a slow dance, but developed into a composition consisting of a bass theme over which other music is heard.

Chorale   A Protestant hymn tune. Bach frequently used them in his choral works.

Chorale Prelude   Chorale adapted for instrumental use, chiefly for the organ.

Chromatic Fantasia and Fugue   A keyboard work by Bach notable for its chromatic (halftone) progressions.

Clavichord   A keyboard instrument with brass strings that were struck by a brass blade at a tangent, giving a light pleasant sound. It was a highly responsive instrument, of great sensitivity and subtlety.

Clavier   Generalized term for keyboard. In Bach's time it could be applied to clavichord, harpsichord, or even organ.

Clavierbüchlein   Or, *Little Clavier Book*. Bach compiled two, one for his young son Wilhelm Friedemann, the other for his wife Anna Magdalena, containing keyboard pieces and songs. They were intended for home instruction and diversion, not publication.

Clavier-Übung   Literally, keyboard exercise. Published in three sections, it contains some of Bach's most notable works for harpsichord and organ.

Concerto   In Bach's time, this term referred to the concerto grosso, an orchestral work in which a small group of instruments (concertino) contrasted with a large group (ripieno, or tutti).

Consistory   Governing board of a church.

English Suites   A set of six harpsichord suites by Bach. The words "fait pour les Anglois" ("made for the English") on an early manuscript suggest that they were commissioned by English patrons.

Fantasia A free-ranging composition in which a composer develops his ideas unrestricted by set forms. In Bach's time, for keyboard rather than orchestra.

French Suites Suites for harpsichord, somewhat more sober than his English suites and generally shorter and simpler. The name is obscure.

Fugue A complex contrapuntal form in which voices enter somewhat in the manner of a canon, but undergo considerable development, variation, and contrast with other musical material. Bach was the supreme master of the form.

Goldberg Variations Thirty variations on a sarabande composed by Bach for performance by a clavier player named Goldberg, whose employer was looking for music to help lighten his sleepless nights.

Harpsichord A keyboard instrument in which the strings are plucked with a quill. The lute-harpsichord is a variant.

Invention Bach may or may not have invented the invention; in any case he raised it to an art—a short keyboard piece in two- or sometimes three-part counterpoint. Often the first "serious" music a neophyte pianist encounters.

Italian Concerto A work for harpsichord with two manuals in part II of the *Clavier-Übung*. Bach described it as "*einem Concerto nach Italienischen Gusto.*"

Magnificat The canticle of the Virgin, sung at vespers in the Roman Catholic rite. Bach's, in D major, is an elaborate but fairly short cantata.

Mass in B minor The mass is the central service of Roman Catholicism, although in treatments by composers from

Bach on it has also taken its place in the concert hall. Lutheran elements infuse Bach's version.

Motet An unaccompanied choral or vocal composition, almost always sacred in nature.

Musical Offering Set of thirteen compositions by Bach on the "Royal Theme" given him by Frederick the Great in 1747.

Oratorio A large-scale composition for voices, chorus, and orchestra on a religious text.

Orgelbüchlein Bach's *Little Organ Book*, containing forty-six chorale preludes, isn't so little.

Overture In Bach's day, a three-movement orchestral work. The French overture was slow-fast-slow, the Italian fast-slow-fast. The works known today as "suites for orchestra" were called overtures by Bach.

Partita A general term for an instrumental composition, more or less equivalent to a suite. An Italian term whose French equivalent is *partie*.

Passacaglia Similar to the chaconne, although the theme need not be in the bass.

Passion A musical setting of one of the gospels, usually of extended length.

Quodlibet A piece made up of several popular tunes combined with imagination and ingenuity—an enjoyable musical practice that has unfortunately died out.

Ricercar A fuguelike contrapuntal composition. The name had nearly gone out of use by Bach's day, but he revived it for his *Musical Offering*.

Sinfonia An orchestral composition in many parts.

Suite An assemblage of instrumental movements based on dance forms, including the allemande, courante, sarabande, gigue, and frequently others. Bach applied it to extended works both for individual instruments, such as clavier, violin, and cello, and for full orchestra.

Toccata From the Italian for "touch." Applied generally to a variety of instrumental pieces.

Well-Tempered Clavier This is Bach's own title for two sets of books each with twenty-four preludes and fugues in all the major and minor keys. Bach composed it to demonstrate the feasibility of "equal temperament"—that is, tuning the keyboard by dividing it into twelve equal semitones so that it could be played readily in any key. The resultant pieces, whose appeal far transcends their didactic purpose, are known familiarly to pianists as "the Forty-eight."

Bach Festivals
in the United States

Following is a list of Bach Festivals in the United States based on data supplied by the American Chapter of the New Bach Society, 1715 Main Street, Bethlehem, Pa. 18018. Date of founding is given where available. The listing is alphabetical by state and city.

Alabama
   Birmingham: Basically Bach (Greater Birmingham Arts Alliance).

California
   Carmel: Carmel Bach Festival (1935).
   Long Beach: Long Beach Bach Festival (1973).
   Los Angeles: Los Angeles Bach Festival (1934).

Colorado
   Boulder: Boulder Bach Festival (1981).
   Fort Collins: Bach Festival at St. Luke's (1978).

District of Columbia
   Ascensiontide Washington Bach Festival (1965).
   Bach Marathon (Chevy Chase Concerts) (1970).

Florida
   Lakeland: Bach Festival of Central Florida (1976).

Pensacola: Christ Church Bach Festival (1980).
Winter Park: Bach Festival Society of Winter Park (Rollins College) (1935).

Georgia
Atlanta: Atlanta Bach Choir.

Iowa
Council Bluffs: Southwest Iowa Bach Festival (1981).

Kentucky
Louisville: Louisville Bach Society (1964).

Michigan
Cass City: Village Bach Festival (1979).
Dearborn: Dearborn Bach Festival (University of Michigan–Dearborn).
Flint: Basically Bach Festival 85.
Kalamazoo: Kalamazoo Bach Festival Society (Kalamazoo College) (1945).

Minnesota
Minneapolis: Bach Society of Minnesota.

Missouri
St. Louis: Bach Society of St. Louis (1941).

New Jersey
Princeton: Westminster College Bach Festival (1985).

New Mexico
Orchestra of Santa Fe Bach Festival (1977).

New York
New York City: Bach to Bach (Chamber Music Society of Lincoln Center) (1984).

Basically Bach (Musica Sacra) (1979).
Brooklyn Bach Festival (1980).
Tureck Bach Institute (1982).
Rochester: Rochester Bach Festival (Rochester Oratorio Society) (1955).
Stony Brook: Bach Aria Festival and Institute (Bach Aria Group) (1981).

North Carolina
Raleigh: North Carolina Bach Festival.

Ohio
Berea: Baldwin-Wallace College Bach Festival (1932).
Dayton: Dayton Bach Society (University of Dayton).

Oregon
Eugene: Oregon Bach Festival (University of Oregon) (1970).
St. Benedict: Abbey Bach Festival (1972).

Pennsylvania
Bethlehem: Bach Choir of Bethlehem (1898).
Philadelphia: Basically Bach Festival of Philadelphia (1976).

Texas
Dallas: Dallas Bach Festival (Southern Methodist University).

Vermont
Brattleboro: New England Bach Festival (1969).

Virginia
Arlington: Washington Bach Consort (1977).

Washington
Spokane: Northwest Bach Festival (1979).

A Brief Bach Bibliography

Spitta, Philipp: *Bach*. Two volumes. New York: Dover Publications, Inc. Bibliographical note by Saul Novack. Published originally from 1873 to 1880, this 1,800-page work remains the most complete and comprehensive of all Bach biographies. (Reprint 1957.)

David, Hans T., and Arthur Mendel: *The Bach Reader: A Life of Johann Sebastian Bach in Letters and Documents*. New York: W. W. Norton & Company. A fascinating and illuminating collection of documents relating to Bach during his life and afterward (1945, rev. 1966). Includes complete text of the first Bach biography by J. N. Forkel (1802).

Geiringer, Karl: *Johann Sebastian Bach: The Culmination of an Era*. New York: Oxford University Press. An excellent modern critical biography (1966).

Terry, Charles Sanford: *The Music of Bach: An Introduction*. New York: Dover Publications, Inc. Brief, concise, intelligible analysis (original publication 1933, reprint 1963).

The Bach Family. Washington, D.C.: Groves' Dictionaries of Music, Inc. A paperback compilation of articles on Bach and his sons extracted from the *New Grove Dictionary of Music and Musicians* (1983).

Holst, Imogen: *Bach*. New York: Thomas Y. Crowell Company. A short, well-illustrated book designed for young readers. Part of "The Great Composers" series (1965).

Acknowledgments

I would like to thank a number of Bach specialists, friends, and colleagues who have made suggestions or given help that has been of benefit to this book. At the same time, I would like to emphasize that none of them shares any responsibility for the shape, form, or contents of the book, not to mention any errors that may have been committed therein. My gratitude, then, to Carol Baron, Samuel Baron, Shirley Burke, David Bury, Alfred Mann, Leslie Meredith, Marguerite Michaels, Blanche Moyse, Gordon Paine, Peter Schickele, and Rosalyn Tureck, as well as members of my own family, who have perhaps received more information about Bach in recent months than they care to remember.

Index

INDEX

INDEX

INDEX

INDEX

INDEX

INDEX

INDEX

About the Author

Herbert Kupferberg is an internationally renowned music critic. Former Lively Arts Editor and record columnist of the *New York Herald Tribune*, he is now a senior editor of *Parade* magazine. His previous books include *Tanglewood*, an illustrated history of America's leading music festival: *Those Fabulous Philadelphians*; *The Mendelssohns*; and *The Book of Classical Music Lists*. He lives in Forest Hills, New York.